FLAGRANTLY ANOREXIC

A MEMOIR
AND
CALL TO ACTION

Lisa Nasseff

Flagrantly Anorexic: A Memoir and Call to Action

www.lisanasseff.com

ISBN (hardcover): 9781642377750

ISBN (paperback): 9781642377767

eISBN: 9781642377774

To my Father, who had unmatched faith in me and my recovery. To the memory of my Mother, whose courage and grace I aspire to. To my Brother, a hero, who cheered me on and on and on.

In Loving Memory of

KATHLEEN ANN

Born

Wednesday, December 31, 1947

Entered into Eternal Life

Saturday, July 2, 2011

Age – 63 Years

Contents

Part Three
Not a Lost Cause

Part Four
A Call to Action

Prologue

My purpose in writing this book is to save lives. I nearly lost mine several times to the demon of anorexia, a scourge that has tormented me for more than thirty years, since the age of ten. I have survived several suicide attempts due to my illness, and I thank my higher power that I am still here to tell you this tale.

For most of my life I have been misunderstood, ridiculed, treated with contempt, and shamed for my eating disorder. I was told by medical professionals that my anorexia was "attention seeking," something I could willfully "control." I was lectured over and over by doctors that my illness was a "choice," an immature indulgence, a condition I could simply "give up," if only I had the character and strength to do so.

At 16 I was committed by court order into a psych ward, accused by the judge of being "flagrantly anorexic." As an adult I suffered the mental torture of being "treated" in an eating disorders clinic, where I was subjected to phony hypnosis therapy that claimed my illness stemmed from childhood sexual abuse and my participation in a satanic cult. Throughout this nightmare I was failed by a negligent insurance "industry" that sanctioned the lunacy of a dysfunctional "mental health system" staffed by incompetent treatment "professionals" who understood neither the complexities of anorexia nor humane and effective ways to treat it.

Despite great fear and trepidation, I decided to write this book so that others battling eating disorders will never be subjected to the nightmares I endured. Doing so was a terribly daunting task. Many times I had to put the book aside, overwhelmed by intolerable memories of the past. Many days I could not face the page, unable to confront my demons. Numerous times I abandoned this book once and for all, certain I would never return to again. But I persevered, convinced that the struggle would be worth the pain if even one person could be helped by this account.

Flagrantly Anorexic is both a memoir and a call to action. It recounts in detail my struggle with anorexia, but in the end it isn't a book about me. It's about the 30 million Americans affected by eating disorders. It's about the inadequate treatment the vast majority of these victims receive. It's about what we need to do to create a mental health system that treats eating disorders with proven, evidence-based treatments rather than with hucksterism and witchcraft. And I say "create" a mental health system rather than "reform," because in my experience we don't have a mental health system. We have to start from scratch by repairing a fragmented approach to providing quality healthcare.

Every 62 minutes at least one person in the U.S. dies from an eating disorder. Nearly half of all Americans know someone with one. Anorexia is not a "condition" and absolutely not a choice—it's a mental illness. Yet research into these illnesses is drastically low. While eating disorders are more prevalent than breast cancer, HIV, and schizophrenia, we spend 300 times more research dollars on those illnesses. U.S. federal funding for eating disorders is $28 million a year, which comes to less than one dollar per person diagnosed with this condition.

I want this book to light a fire under lawmakers. Our Congress and all elected officials work for us—for all Americans. Never forget that. This is a crisis that can't be ignored. We need a mental health system now! We need enforcement of laws and valid accountability now! We need vigilant oversight and evidence-based care now! We need a revolution in how we treat all mental illnesses.

After more than thirty years in hell, I've come to accept me as I am. No longer embarrassed and ashamed by the hand that was dealt to me, I have discovered a freedom that I never knew before. I have found my voice and I am using it to ask you, the reader, to join with me and help fight this crusade. We need to use all our voices. Together.

I know there is hope. If you have been a casualty too, please don't give up. I never did. No one is a lost cause—no one. Let's fight for the treatment and dignity we deserve.

I hope you can hear me.

Lisa Nasseff

Sept. 1, 2019

Part One

Mirror, Mirror on the Wall

Chapter One

Think Happier Thoughts

My heart was pounding through my chest and my legs were cramping up. Couldn't stand—if I had tried, I would have faded to black. So sick I had to crawl like an animal from the bathroom to my bedroom, where I could only sit on the floor. No energy to climb on the bed. Mom sat with me, her arm draped around my shoulders.

The sound of the sirens rising higher and higher. Louder and louder. Closer and closer. I couldn't breathe. Was I beyond the point of no return?

The bright lights inside the ambulance were blinding as I lay on my back and they fired question after question at me. "What were you thinking?" they demanded with contempt. "Why would you do this?"

I hadn't committed a felony; I simply took too many laxatives. And now I was making my first trip to the emergency room for anorexia, at age 13.

Suddenly they were scrambling around inside the ambulance. My heart was misfiring and my blood pressure was terribly low. The sirens echoed inside my brain. I cried *please stop*, *don't make me fat* as they poured liquids through my veins and gave me a huge shot of something. They babbled in a language I didn't understand, never looking me in the face.

"How many calories does this stuff have?" I demanded.

My pleas were ignored. Lying there terrified with the wires, the beeping, and the anger that permeated every bit of space. My panic left unnoticed as I feared for my life.

We arrived. Glaring bright lights pierced my brain. The corridor filled with white light. Doctors, nurses, and staff crisscrossing everywhere in this cold maze. Every corner and corridor looked the same. Gray floors and white walls.

What have I done? What is happening? Why such anger directed at me?

The inflatable balloon pants were next, squeezing my legs oh so tight to increase my blood pressure.

Would someone talk to me please? I'm right here!

The doctor stormed in, shouting. "We have people who need to be treated because they're sick! Not because *they make themselves sick!*"

Explaining nothing about the wires, the pants,

and what were they putting inside my body—I was supposed to be in charge of that! After an eternity, a nurse came in to check the machines. Not a look or a word. The doctor arrived again, still furious. Why was I wasting their time?

"You don't look like you have an eating disorder. These attention seeking antics could be fatal! I hope you learned a lesson!"

The tears came on and I thought they would never stop. An attention seeking gimmick? I wanted to disappear—all the time. I felt disgust for my body, along with shame and guilt. I hid in oversized clothes, pushed people away, and rarely left the house.

I was repulsive and unlovable. I would never admit to hunger because I was ferociously afraid of food, afraid that I would lose control and eat everything in sight. This fear inhabited my every thought.

I was held for 72 hours, rehydrated, and sent home, where the cycle started all over again.

Our family dinners had become a war zone. My parents' rules were that I had to sit at the table until I finished my plate. I had until 8 p.m. to do so.

I considered this punitive, but they must have thought setting a deadline was the only way to help me. Sometimes I sat there for almost two hours after they had already left the table, silent and defiant, roiled by anger and resentment, while they did their post-dinner chores around me. Sometimes as she passed by mom would say to me, "Lisa, why are you doing this?"

I stared at my plate—a large white plate with peas scattered about. With my knife I tried to herd them into close proximity, but they rolled in different directions, intent on ignoring my wishes. I couldn't bear to eat a single one. The idea repulsed me, made me nauseous from fear, not lack of hunger. I tried once again to herd them into a group; once again they defied me. I glanced at the clock. I could wait it out until 8 p.m. My only thought was to defy my hunger, or to chew my food and spit it into my napkin until the deadline passed and I was free.

But I was never free.

Mirror, mirror on the wall, who's the thinnest of them all? Mirrors didn't lie. I scrutinized myself in them, made disparaging comments about my body, compared my shape and size to those of others. A person with anorexia can look in the mirror and see a reflection that is greater than her actual size. I never would have believed this if I had not experienced it firsthand, over and over again. A friend of mine once had me try on her jeans, as I was sure I was bigger than she was. They fell to the floor. I was confused, shocked. But the mirror didn't lie.

It wasn't that I didn't like food. I was terrified of it. Terrified of liking it. Terrified of hunger. Terrified of losing control and gaining weight.

I would intentionally eat things I couldn't stomach, food I didn't like. Soup right out of the can, as punishment for my hunger. Eating rituals soothed my discomfort and uncertainty, offering the illusion of stability, reliability, and control. My rules were many, rigid, and unforgiving.

One of them was to eat only one thing at a time. Foods couldn't be mixed. On Thanksgiving I had to eat the stuffing first before I ate turkey or mashed potatoes. Had to eat at the same time every day, organizing everything around that time. Soon I couldn't eat in public and eventually not in the presence of anyone, not even my family.

By age 13 I had experienced nearly every symptom of anorexia. Amenorrhea, or lack of menstruation. I don't think I ever had a regular flow. Elevated liver enzymes. Dizziness and fainting. Hair loss, which was devastating. Dry skin. Intolerance of cold—all the time. Irregular heart rhythms with very low blood pressure. Dehydration over and over again. But my rules never wavered.

Yes, I was a lost cause, losing control over the very thing I was trying so frantically to control. Relentless fear and self-loathing with no relief in sight. My boat wandering adrift with no energy to row, no verve to fight this fight. In grave danger, sinking fast and furiously, with too much weight to carry. I was not equipped for white water rafting, nor was my boat. Could I throw this baggage overboard? Alone? Not a chance.

My eating disorder spoke another language. I was unable to receive compliments. When someone said "You're looking good" or "You look healthy," that meant I was fat. "What did you do today?" was an accusation that I was lazy or just a waste of skin. People were dishonest when they said I was too thin; I was certain I was not. I became suspicious, losing all trust. With my self-hatred running so deep, every intention and word meant failure.

"Just deal with it—eat."

"Lisa, everyone feels this way sometimes."

"We've all been there."

"Maybe try thinking happier thoughts."

Everyone feels this way? Just think happier thoughts?

If only they could be in my shoes and hear these words.

My first day of kindergarten. Mom fixed my wild hair into big smooth curls, and we put on my new red dress with navy blue embroidery down the front. White tights and patent leather shoes. I was ready for class pictures as we packed up to go, excited but also nervous that my classmates wouldn't like me. Always a very anxious child, always feeling the sadness of others as deeply as my own. So sensitive that even as a young child I couldn't watch the news. The many tragedies left me devastated.

And sensitive to people's bodies. I was only three when I told my mom she had a fat butt, but not to worry because it was "only in the back." My cousin later told me that I would point out people who were "really big" when I was at the library or shopping, which really embarrassed mom. I have no idea where that came from.

The wind tossed my curls as we drove the few blocks to Catholic school. The leaves were changing to brilliant reds and oranges. Mom had over-prepared me for anything I could encounter—Kleenex, Band-Aids, pencils, a sharpener, little erasers in the shapes of animals. Things I didn't even need, but she thought of everything.

My mom was born to be a mom. Our friends called her June Cleaver, the principle character in the American television sitcom *Leave It to Beaver*. June and her husband Ward were the archetypal suburban parents of the 1950s.

We were everything to her, me and my little brother Mike. Her birthday parties were the talk of the town. Always a new birthday dress for me. She invited friends and foes alike, and everyone came because they knew Mrs. Nasseff put on a great show—gift bags, great food, fun games, and the Master of Ceremonies took charge of it all. She was a marvelous cook and baker, famous at school bake sales for her cookies on a stick. She was good and pure and had love for everyone who crossed her path. Yes, we got on each other's nerves, but that was mostly me. Me and my ED.

From a very early age I craved perfection. To be

the absolute best. I failed if I couldn't achieve my self-imposed goals. Getting a B on a test filled me with shame and self-hate.

I started dancing when I was four, dreaming of those graceful ballerinas floating across the stage with seeming ease. Mom was a master at making my costumes, the tutus and the blue leotard.

And, of course, tap and jazz too. I loved tap dancing! I felt free—the rhythm you could create while the mistakes went unnoticed. Jazz was a little too embarrassing for me, too dramatic. It left me feeling exposed. Ballet was very disciplined, nothing like I had imagined, requiring meticulous control over my body's movements. But I loved the ballet bar and the mirror that traced my every move, never imagining the mirror would turn on me with dreadful effects.

I remember dancing for the governor with my fur coat and a hat that was so much bigger than I was, Vegas style. Balancing the monstrosity on my head, afraid I would fail. Embarrassing everyone who knew me.

My Catholic school uniform was a green plaid dress with patent leather shoes; they made us kneel to make sure our skirts reached the floor. And, oh my goodness, our priest was larger than life and the most petrifying man I had met thus far. His voice booming as he walked down the aisle of the church. We attended Mass every Sunday and I learned to fear God and sin and hell. I always mouthed the singing as my voice was abysmal, which the Father confirmed, shouting, "Let's hear it—He gave it to you, now you can give it right back." He reminded me of Darth Vader, shaking his head with disappointment as he looked down at me. If I could have done so without upsetting God, I would have crawled under the pew.

It wasn't until fourth grade that I became a "social butterfly." I wanted everyone to like me, craving popularity so badly that I was awful to a few classmates. That's not how I was raised; everything we were taught was black and white. But I forgot— was teasing other kids a mortal or a venial sin? Guilt and shame when confronted by my mother. I made it worse by lying, more evidence that I was a sinner. Appalled and humiliated. All I wanted was to be liked, but more seeds of self-hatred had been planted.

It was also in fourth grade I started playing the trombone, soon switching to clarinet like the other girls (I couldn't make a sound with the flute). I loved the band conductor, but since I wasn't the best I gave it little effort. But he understood that: "You'll never be first chair without practicing." I was breathing through my nose, which was unacceptable, so he had me put cotton balls in my nostrils and they shot right out. I laughed even though it wasn't very funny.

I was horrible in gym. Always the last to be picked. Always so embarrassed. That's when I first began feeling uncomfortable changing in front of others. I had matured faster than my peers and it was demoralizing. I worried about my body constantly and this only fueled my self-hatred. "You're a fat pig," I told myself.

One day in fifth grade class, when I was nine, that self-hate was confirmed. I was sitting at my desk when the boy behind me poked me with his pencil. When I turned around, he called me a fat pig. Why, I have no idea. I asked the teacher if I could go to the bathroom, so devastated that I slammed the door on the way out. The classroom clock fell off the wall.

I sat in the bathroom and cried. My fears had been realized—I *was* a fat pig and everyone knew it.

I was only 10 when the mirrors turned on me. I was at the ballet bar and looked at my body from the side. My stomach protrudcd from my red and blue-striped leotard with the fancy blue belt. I looked at the other girls and theirs were flat. And my legs were way too big, out of proportion with my body. Instant repulsion. I would never be a ballerina. I was fat and had to lose weight. The battle had begun.

I turned to drawing and my teachers found that I had some talent. Drew the yearbook covers and for art shows. Even my science projects were a work of art. My mom and I would spend hours together as I shared my ideas and she helped me bring them to life. One of my favorites was—how ironic—a digestive system that I carved from styrofoam, using playdoh to sculpt the inner organs.

Again, perfection always the goal. Anxious by nature? Or because perfection was elusive, always beyond my grasping reach? Questions I still can't answer.

School was supposed to be easy—allegedly I was gifted. But mostly I felt a failure and fat. I hated home economics. I could never imagine being a wife. Never dreamt of being a bride. Instead, I wanted to change the world. But how? I had always felt things so deeply, and couldn't stop the pain and darkness that were creeping up on me. How could I save the world if I couldn't save myself?

Enter Neil Diamond (for real). His lyrics were singing my song. I listened and listened and listened; I was sure he understood me. His eyes were rich with emotion. Wrote letters asking if he would adopt me. I went to his concerts with my aunt and was awestruck by all the people cheering as he glided across the stage dancing to the music. Telling my story with words that I couldn't articulate. To this day the most talented songwriter—ever! I wanted to make people happy like Neil did. He sparkled like a star—my star.

Have you ever had a song in your head you couldn't let go? Soon, my song was all I could hear—food, calories, weight, and exercise. I was unbearably miserable. A darkness, a black depression that I struggled to explain. By age 12 I was using laxatives to purge myself. By age 14 I wouldn't change my clothes or shower for days in a row. Avoiding the body I had treated with disdain. Getting out of bed was beyond my capacity. Too exhausted. When I did, it drained me for hours afterward.

I longed for my family to understand the darkness that encircled me. Obsessed that people could see the panic and fear in my eyes—the window to my soul.

Afraid of leaving the house, of answering the phone, of looking in the mirror.

Obsession from the time I woke up in the morning until the time I went to bed at night. *Fat and Skinny had a race, all around the pillowcase. Fat fell down and Skinny won the race.* Anxiety off the charts and frightening depression. Every thought, word, and movement was an effort. Not laziness. Not lack of will. Not attention getting. Not a choice. I was malnourished, isolated, brimming with self-hate and unrelenting fear, something I couldn't fix on my own. Dancing with death. Dancing with a stranger.

My mind was always racing. Exhausting and overwhelming, like pressing on the gas and the brakes at the same time. Like watching a movie in another language with no subtitles. Like having the radio on high and trying to read. Food—weight—fear. No reprieve, just madness, as the hours crawled by.

My dad was angry; he thought my behavior was a cry for attention. My mom was confused but trying hard to break through to me. Without much success.

I had become an accomplished anorexic who wanted to be the best. My friend had anorexia and I was jealous of her success. So I mastered all the tricks and how to mask them. Diet aids, exercising excessively, the constant lies. Chanted "*I don't need food, I don't need food, I am fat, I am fat*" as I ran on the treadmill. Dressed to hide my condition. Abused massive amounts of laxatives. Stole money from my family to purchase them. What did the lady behind the counter think, seeing me every other day, my head lowered in shame?

But my "solution" turned on me, stealing all reason and reality. The laxatives cleaned out my feelings along with everything else. With my emotions numb, I made reprehensible decisions. Wounding many people in my path. Never fitting in but always trying to change myself to do so. I had lost my identity, if I ever had one. I thought I *was* my eating disorder; I couldn't see myself with any objectivity or proportion.

High school was Catholic, as had been grade school and junior high. This led to a series of calamitous events. I begged and pleaded to go to public school, where all my friends went. A resolute NO was the answer. However, I was able to circumvent the all-girls school by reluctantly deciding on another Catholic high school in the area, a smaller one not far from home with an accelerated track. It had an accomplished marching band and a struggling dance line.

Marching band practice in the heat of the summer. Relearning the trombone rather quickly, so I could be in the front line. *Dress left dress!* A sharp look to the left, so embarrassed of the body I had dressed to hide. My contradiction—I wanted to be perfect but I didn't want to be seen. Exposed in my black polyester uniform, with a hat resembling a large white fedora. Soon learned about a powerful diuretic in the medicine cabinet. So powerful I could lose several pounds in just hours. Those pounds crept right back just as quickly.

The band traveled each year to various locations across the country; it was a challenge to fit in while immersed in my quest to disappear. But I could always fake being more together and excited than I was. I did this well—too well.

Schoolwork was not thought-provoking. Thank goodness, as the space in my head was rather limited. My pursuit for perfection led to more extracurricular activities. Soon joined the dance line, giving performances and entering competitions. Became a choreographer in my junior year and then co-captain my senior year. We practiced every day. Dreading competitions, as our attire didn't hide much. Therefore, more starving, more laxatives, more diuretics. And more lies.

Keeping up with the rigorous practices soon became a challenge that I couldn't meet. My depression became apparent; my dark days were increasing rapidly. I overheard our vice-principal say sarcastically as I passed in the hallway, "What's wrong with Lisa now?" But no compassion or concern or follow-up from him. I was a joke.

In my junior year of high school, my friend and I were both chosen to go to New York City to try out as models for an agency. We were standing right outside the gym when my friend delighted in telling me that the modeling agency thought my weight was a problem even though they had accepted me. My friend's mother had apparently snuck into my file to find out that private information. I hadn't known we were in a competition. This incident sent me into a downward spiral, and I ended up not going to New York because my eating disorder kicked up again.

I was friends with different groups or cliques, of varied interests and depth. I harbored a deep desire to be liked by everyone and yearned to be in the "popular" group. When I began dating a college student in my junior year, I felt I fit in a bit more.

Nevertheless, that wasn't enough, and I soon began to self-medicate. Smoking pot and trying alcohol. The latter had calories, so I was careful and didn't need much. I was the girl the teachers asked to check the bathroom for smokers. I'd have a few puffs before reporting back. I didn't know how to smoke, which is how I met one of my very best friends who had the pleasure of teaching me. After several months I learned that my friend also had a drinking problem with serious suicidal ideation. I understood that ideation all too well. We became closer as we shared our misery.

I confided in her about my struggle, as I had overdosed once before when I was 13 from taking Tylenol. It wasn't a serious attempt. Didn't want to die, but it was too painful to live. She also had a couple of suicide attempts, labeled as "attention seeking." Her desperation overlooked. Her begging for help.

We made a pact. If one of us committed suicide, the other would soon follow. This friend went into treatment for alcohol and my parents forbade me to be her friend. I was crushed, but got around that rule once she was out. We made ourselves available to each other in our secret ways. Six weeks later she hung herself, April 20th, 1986. She was 15.

I was sure it was my fault. The school announcement was cold and matter of fact. I overheard a classmate say, "Now her druggie friends will be moping around." A few of us left school, overwhelmed with sadness at the news.

I remember seeing my psychiatrist, Dr. Doom, a few days later, so sick and dehydrated that I was barely able to walk into his office. As I lay down on his couch, he inquired about why my symptoms were so severe. My mom was with me because I was so sick. We shared that my best friend had just committed suicide. Dr. Doom simply said "Oh" and moved on to another subject with no reaction at all. Had he heard me? Could anyone hear me?

One of my friends confronted me, telling me our friend's suicide was my fault because I knew of the previous attempts and because she had started giving me her things. I couldn't breathe. Already overwhelmed with guilt, our "friend" only confirmed it. I had nightmares for months, as my bestie's image floated outside my bedroom window, seated Indian-style, staring at me. Tormented by my biggest failure yet. Why hadn't she called me? Why? My heart ached with a pain so deep that it took me over completely.

I never kept my end of the pact. Or perhaps I did—starving, laxatives, diuretics. Killing myself slowly.

I was a master of pretending to be okay, but pretending could only go so far. I couldn't hide any longer. At ages 14 and 15 I made thirteen trips to the emergency room. After the last trip I wasn't discharged after I stabilized, which was the usual routine, but was instead sent to the psychiatric ward, terribly depressed and irrational. Dr. Doom, my psychiatrist, said to me, "You're dangerously dehydrated and we're trying to save your life. Why are you doing this to yourself?"

You tell me, Dr. Doom. Why?

He had no answer and neither did I. I cared about nothing and no one. I existed only to count calories, exercise, and lose weight.

Dr. Doom was on a rampage. He had no understanding of eating disorders. He thought my symptoms resulted from repressed memories of sexual abuse and was relentless in convincing me of this fact.

"Do it!" Dr. Doom demanded. "Remember what happened to you. Just do what I say."

Just cooperate with his treatment and follow instructions. But what was I supposed to do exactly? Remember something that never happened? Or had I forgotten it? All my symptoms indicated sexual abuse, Dr. Doom said. But by whom? My dad? Had he abused me and I didn't remember?

First I was defiant; then I wondered whether Dr. Doom was right.

Anger, so much anger. *Just eat. Just remember the abuse. Do it!* My symptoms, he told me, were too grave not to have deep-seated roots. Repressed memories, he told me over and over again, were the cause. But I couldn't remember anything. I was a hopeless case, only confirming my fears that I was innately broken and hopeless.

I was just 15 years old. A child.

Chapter Two

Flagrantly Anorexic

I learned from another patient that I could sign myself out of the psych ward when I turned 16. That was the day I waited for, as they probed me for repressed memories that were the root of my illness.

I barely listened as Dr. Doom droned on about the eating regimen I should observe at home once I was discharged. In the middle of our session, a man stuck his head in the office.

"Are you Lisa Nasseff? You've been served." He handed me a slip of paper—a court order revoking my pending discharge and petitioning the court to commit me to the hospital indefinitely beyond age 16. Signed by mom. Dr. Doom had gotten her to do this without a word spoken to me.

Anger surged through my veins, blinding me. My shrink's lips were moving but I heard nothing. I don't know what stopped me from ripping the papers to shreds and throwing them in his face. Why had they betrayed me? Why hadn't my family talked to me? Why couldn't I be freed from jail?

My dad had never understood my eating disorder. He thought I was choosing to destroy myself. With allegations of sexual abuse floating around, we had stopped talking. Only my mom gave me any semblance of support and understanding. And now she did this? Unable to contain my rage, I stormed out of my shrink's office and bolted to my room. That night I tossed and turned, haunted by the same incessant demons that never left my mind. Would I ever be normal? Would anyone ever understand what I was going through?

Committing me to the psych ward was a legal proceeding and I was called before a judge. It was utterly unreal, as if I were being called to judgment for a crime I had forgotten. The judge lectured me from the bench, which towered over me, larger than life. I will never forget that moment.

"You're being committed," he said angrily, "because you are flagrantly anorexic."

Had I really heard those words? So poisonous they pierced me to the core. Was someone with depression "flagrantly depressed"? Was a person with cancer "flagrantly cancerous"? As judge and executioner, his one word summed up all the ways I had been mistreated for years—belittled, blamed, and completely misunderstood.

Over the next few days, the nightmare intensified. The staff told me I had a "choice"—if I followed the program in the hospital, they wouldn't commit me to the state mental institution. But what program? I was in a hospital that didn't know anything about eating disorders. I was thrown in with the general psych population, people with all kinds of severe mental illnesses that I didn't understand any more than they understood mine. My roommate scared me; in a fit of rage, she had tried to murder her mom. Holy shit!

I had an eating disorder and major depression, which they treated by feeding me, period. I was forced to eat three balanced meals; a staff person sat next to me to make sure I didn't confiscate anything. They weighed me every morning; if I hadn't gained half a pound from the previous day, I was confined to my room between meals. Solitary confinement for anorexia! But the isolation didn't bother me. Much preferred to the various groups that never addressed the disease that had claimed my life.

They continued to instill in me that the severity of my eating disorder meant that I had suffered sexual abuse earlier in my life. Every day I met with Dr. Doom.

"Let's think back to when you were a child," he asked once again. "Was your dad ever inappropriate with you?"

"What are you talking about?" I responded. "Inappropriate how?"

"Lisa, did he ever touch you in an inappropriate way? Or have any other physical contact with you that was inappropriate?"

"I've told you—no!"

"Are you sure? Or could it be that you don't remember? Try to think back."

The reality was that I didn't have memories of *any* physical contact from my dad, not even a hug.

I dreaded my therapy sessions. The tension enveloped me. I was either fighting with Dr. Doom or not saying much. He interrogated me like a suspect in a police precinct. *You've got to get in touch with your feelings. We have to figure this out, so you can get out of the hospital.* This went on for months on end.

It soon became clear what would get me out—I had to say what they wanted to hear. Might it be possible that I had been sexually abused and just didn't remember? Maybe it had happened. I began to believe it. It was a terrifying feeling not to know the truth, to have no memory of something so profound. Was this why I had been starving myself? A deep depression gripped me again. It was my fault, my failing, my moral weakness, to have allowed myself to be abused and to not remember it.

Dr. Doom would get me into a relaxed state and say, "Let's think back to when you were a child."

I didn't know how to answer him. I didn't understand the concept of repressed memory, which was the subject of almost all of our individual sessions.

They had me see another therapist, because they thought it might be easier for me to talk to a female. "You have to start eating and gain weight," she said, as if I were a misbehaving child. She tapped her pencil against her legal pad impatiently and waited for me to respond. I kept staring at her red blouse, unable to meet her judging gaze. It seemed like we went back and forth over the same territory, had the same conversation, day after day after day. Why couldn't they hear me?

I vividly remember saying to Dr. Doom, "What happens if the sexual abuse isn't true and I'm just crazy?"

He said, "Well, that would be easier to treat."

What did that mean? Easier to treat if I were full-blown crazy? What did that say about my condition?

My unwavering fears around food plagued me every day. Whenever I was in the dining room, I was terrified I would lose control and start eating. And if I started eating I was petrified that I wouldn't be able to stop, that I would gain and gain and gain. That was always the core fear, the primordial fear, the fear that never deserted me.

My body and my eating took up all of my thinking, when I wasn't being asked to dive into past memories that weren't there. Months went by and their questions never changed.

"Are you sure you don't remember? Because that's what everything's pointing to. Think back to when you were young. What was your father like around you?"

What compounded the problem was that I had family therapy in the hospital with my parents, where the sexual abuse theory was openly discussed. The first time it was mentioned, my dad stalked out of the room and my mom and I went into hysterics. I had to uncover the sexual abuse and get to the magic weight number to get out of the hospital, but I couldn't do either.

Sometimes I wouldn't finish my food and I'd have to sit in the dining room after everyone was gone. They became frustrated when I cut everything into little pieces to forestall the process and keep them waiting. Back in my room the panic hit me—how I could burn it off? I ran in place, did pushups, sit ups, leg lifts, anything to consume the calories.

Some of the other patients became envious of the attention I was getting. Like my dad, they believed my ED was a manipulative, attention-getting mechanism . My roommate told me what the other patients were saying—that I wasn't eating so I could get more attention. Sometimes people said that in group therapy, although none of them had an ED.

I dreaded the attention. I wanted to disappear.

They experimented with giving me passes home, letting me leave for a night or weekend. My relationship with my parents was very strained. How could it not? I was sleeping in a house where my dad might have done something to me and my mom may have covered it up. I contemplated running away, but where would I go?

When I reverted back to my behaviors and lost weight while out on a pass, that privilege was revoked. Why would they send me home in the first place if they had believed that was the genesis of my eating disorder? None of my problems were being treated in a logical, credible way. We just kept going around and around in a dizzying, never-ending circle.

My court-ordered commitment to the hospital was open-ended, at the discretion of the doctor. I was about to turn 16 and could have been committed indefinitely. Missing school and my friends was not on my radar; my sole fixation was on getting out. It got to the point where I said to my therapists, "*Help me remember it. Please, help me to remember!*" I started having dreams that seemed like flashbacks. I was a young child and someone was in my bedroom. I was overcome by anxiety, wondering if I should reveal my dreams in therapy. If I did, what would happen to my family?

I was a wreck. I had no answers. I didn't understand my obsessions and compulsions, and never had. I thought my fingers were too chubby. I was even afraid to lick envelopes and stamps. Would I ever leave the psych ward?

Nearly a year passed. I couldn't spend another week there. I asked my therapist, "What do I need to do? Is it possible something happened and I'll never remember it?"

Her response: "It could be."

I never gave them a specific memory of sexual abuse, but I did tell them the truth—that I was scared to sleep in my bed at home starting when I was a young child. Instead, I'd sleep on the floor in my parents' bedroom. That could have been an attachment issue, but my therapists thought it was highly peculiar and evidence of their theory.

I was giving them something to work with, even if it didn't make sense—if my dad was abusing me, why would I sleep on the floor in my parents' bedroom? Seek comfort in a dangerous den?

What finally got me out was hitting the magic weight number and my willingness to do family therapy upon discharge. I gave them what they wanted: the clear message that I might have been abused and that I was going to get to the bottom of it with mom and dad.

At this point my relationship with my dad was ruined. He didn't yell, but he was a very intense person with a look on his face that could be piercing. I thought it was obvious that he was very disappointed in me, convinced my illness was an attempt to win attention. It became harder to be around him. We weren't talking that much to begin with because he worked nights; now we just passed each other in the halls. Before we had been at odds because of my eating disorder; now it was because of something far more disturbing. So disturbing that I apparently couldn't remember it.

Chapter Three

Glory Road

My parents and I went to a handful of therapy sessions together but we didn't spend much time exploring an accusation that none of us thought was true.

Senior year. When I came out of the bathroom one day, a teacher hugged me and said I had been elected Homecoming Queen by a landslide. "Fix your hair nice," she said, "it smells like smoke." It was from the other girls in the bathroom, I assured her.

My feelings were mixed. Mom was a homecoming queen, so I was excited to follow in her footsteps. Did being elected mean that people liked me? Perhaps, but it also meant more attention and I was a fat pig. As we rode around in the car during the football game's half time, waving at the crowd, I was self-conscious as hell in my dance line costume.

I finished my high school credits and graduated. I took a year off before starting college but quickly relapsed once I got there. Although "relapse" might not be the word because I was never healthy, had never been properly treated. And so I teetered on the edge. Another near death experience in the company of friends. Saved by tireless paramedics and emergency care.

For the first time I truly realized my mortality. Watching them work on me as if it were a scene from a bad movie, seeing myself from above as I floated away. No more laxatives, I vowed—ever. Instead, I continued to self-medicate—pot, cocaine, alcohol, prescription pain meds, even LSD. Anything to numb my unrelenting pain. Horrible choices over and over again. More lies and deception. More guilt and shame.

I dropped out of college and had a great deal of trouble finding a decent job without my degree. Self-medicating every day. Wasted. Anorexia was like a drug—I got a high from starving. It made me feel like Wonder Woman when I could lose weight while others struggled, and I kept trying to get that feeling back. Like I was stronger than everyone else because I knew how to control and deny. To defy hunger cues and basic physiological needs and still carry on—a functional anorexic. Facing down temptation as I walked the tightropes of food and weight.

I found a job as a real estate closer, which I knew

nothing about, with the help of my cousin's girlfriend. They were so busy I had to learn in the line of fire, which is how I learned most everything. I went back to college at night. Hitting my rhythm at work, making as much as I could in this field. I couldn't do any more closings. Not enough hours in the day.

So began my quest to pursue a more meaningful career, to right social injustices, to attack racism and poverty, to fix what was broken. I was always for the underdog. Politics! Lawmakers! Social change! I was studying sociology and urgently wanted to work for the mayor of our city. He was inspiring and going places, and I wanted to be a part of it.

Soon I had a job working for him, a place on the inside with rich and powerful people who made big decisions. A ride on Glory Road. I met donors and high ranking public figures, including Presidents Clinton and George W. Bush. It was amusing to be underestimated time after time and then blow their socks off.

My dad would always caution me as I was too enamored by these folks: "They all put their pants on one leg at a time." But from where I was looking, these people had no rules and no limitations. At least none that I could see.

Money talks. But it don't sing and dance and it don't walk.

Again, Neil Diamond. Spot on!

I was dating a lawyer who I loved right away. I also fell in love with my wedding dress on first sight—a perfect dress with spaghetti straps and a beaded bodice blending gold and white beads, which wrapped over my neckline and sparkled as I moved about the store. The bottom had layers and layers of tulle, like Cinderella's dress. I always fell in love before looking at the price. Another father, looking at the price tag, would have told me to send it back. Not mine. We found a tiara that matched perfectly. My uncle's wife, who helped plan the event with every detail of a ball, insisted on a veil and long white gloves. After all, I was a bride—the star of the show, she said. I wanted my hair up but was swayed to keep my curly locks running down my back. My centerpiece flowers were my favorite, white tulips. And our meal was Lebanese, wonderful for all. Who doesn't like garlic?

I felt like a princess. The champagne reception was held in a club rich with history and beauty everywhere you turned. We had a violinist making magic as everyone arrived and throughout dinner. Magical.

Enough of that. It saddens me to think of the

eventual outcome. Like I said, I looked at the price tag after I fell in love.

From the outside looking in, it appeared I was walking on Glory Road. But soon I was self-medicating again. From stage left came Xanax, purchased off the internet. It managed my anxiety, even helped to lessen my underlying self-doubt and self-hatred. Again, more lies. Alcohol reduced my inhibitions under the guise of networking and work-related folly. Wined and dined with the big wigs. Soon I wasn't impressed. It wasn't what I had dreamed about. The so-called brilliance of the rich and famous was an illusion. The magic of social change and making a difference wasn't there. My dreams were extinguished, the fires of my desire snuffed out.

I had the opportunity to be the city's Y2K manager. I enjoyed a unique relationship with the fire department and absorbed a wealth of knowledge through training at FEMA; I attended additional emergency management conferences as well. On seeing that I was conducting a training, a firefighter said to me in disgust: "This is how important this is to the mayor?" I didn't respond but felt crushed to be underestimated again.

I was then hired by a local public relations firm as their chief operating officer, to restructure and turn around a low-performing company that had one large client keeping them afloat. Responsible for identifying weaknesses, and providing strategic and performance planning. I designed and executed (with my talented staff) public relations/marketing strategies promoting brand awareness in the community. Something didn't smell right, however. The firm was sold to an accountant who knew nothing about public relations and he paid an extraordinary amount. The bad smell became stronger. I had to trust my gut and move on. I and two other very intelligent women started our own public relations and audiovisual production firm, bringing previous clients with us.

But enough of my resume talk. Beneath this outward success, my eating disorder was percolating. Not eating for days and passing out in a client's office. Unrelenting embarrassment. More lies and more Xanax. Looking from the outside in, I was still walking Glory Road. I didn't look like I had an eating disorder. Not yet, anyway.

Soon I was asked to be on several non-profit boards. I was delighted and couldn't say no. I jumped in with both feet. Started on the board of a local children's' organization; served on the executive committee; chaired the government relations committee;

delivered nationwide presentations on "Energizing Your Board." I served on our film and television board, the local police department foundation board, as well as on a local hospital foundation board where I co-chaired the annual wine auction fundraiser. Savoring the benefits of extraordinary friends who still grace my life.

So much fun. My husband showed little to no interest. I mostly attended our events with my friends and colleagues. His love was the cabin. Every weekend. My non-profit work experiences fed my soul. I was making a difference. Unfortunately, that was all that was being fed.

An old client of ours committed suicide, a client who kept the previous firm afloat. With my old boss soon to follow, within a year. The horror of it all. My depression tugged hard on my suit and my heightened anxiety needed more Xanax. My self-medicating and anorexia were destroying what I had worked so hard to achieve. I wasn't fooling anyone with my wit and lies.

I preferred to be numb rather than face my

reality. My anorexia soothed my discomfort, stress, uncertainty, pain, and sadness but it didn't take long for it to turn on me, once again. I lost the very control I yearned for and my façade quickly fell apart. *Heeeere's ED!*

"So what are you doing," people would ask. "How are you?" My retort was swift—*stalking Neil Diamond and fighting his restraining order.* Followed by their laughter and changing of the subject, as most people like to talk about themselves anyway. But it never failed. Neil Diamond was my shtick. I had become friends with his percussionist, King Errisson, and to this day we remain dear friends. A silver lining. I met King at the finest hotel in the city where Neil and his band stayed. King and a few others were at the bar. I quickly ran over. He was my favorite, the showman of the band. He kissed me on the forehead after my gushing and said I was too young to be such a fan. No way! I was in my mid-twenties. We had breakfast before the band left and have remained friends ever since. King was always calm; I wished I could take in the world the same way.

As I searched for a rebound, I started a company to provide a new way of funding independent films that would benefit the non-profit world. While I got things started, they never reached completion. No amount of Xanax or starving was going to help me out of the mess I had created. I couldn't think or feel. My mood was becoming too dark to manage; my ability to relate to others waned and soon I couldn't function. And so came the end of Glory Road—stuck in a small pond with very big fish and a few sharks as well.

All I wanted was to disappear. And I did. From everyone and everything. Never leaving the house. The drapes pulled. Afraid to check the messages on our phone. Only by the ticking of the grandfather clock did I know that time was passing while mine stood still.

Part Two

I Didn't Choose This

Chapter Four

Love on the Rocks

I had a fairy tale wedding but the fairy tale ended there. I had been terribly anxious heading into the marriage. An illness had ravaged much of my life, was still lurking beneath the surface, and now I was sharing that life and illness with another person. The tone was set on our honeymoon. I had had a terrifying flight the week before, and the resulting anxiety never went away even after we arrived in the paradise of St. John's, where I tried so hard to manage my fear.

I later told my lawyer that I was the world's worst wife. I was definitely a handful and the first year was most difficult. I had become very jealous of everything. Not being a lawyer like my husband. Being his second wife. Envious of the ex-wife who came with the deal and asserted her presence quite well in our new home and life. Years younger, filled with a troubling insecurity, I was not equipped to deal with these unforeseen emotions.

When we came home from our honeymoon, I found

a dunk tank in our backyard for their son's birthday. The ex-wife took charge of the party—in my home. She invited her friends to the party—in my home. They didn't even look at me—in my home. I hadn't known of her plans and she showed me no deference. Of course I understood she was the mother of my husband's wonderful little boy, and having a step-son was a wonderful gift, but this was over the top right from the start, something I wasn't prepared for. I was angry with my husband that he continued to allow his ex-wife to be so intrusive, ignoring the impact it was having on me. I was a new step-mom. Unchartered territory. And yet having a step-son was a cherished gift.

Most everyone I met through my husband was a lawyer. I wasn't as impressed with them as they were with themselves. I just didn't measure up professionally, which my husband soon pointed out on more than one occasion. Without a post-graduate degree, I felt "less than." In my very first phone call with my future husband, he touted his neighborhood as having a very high percentage of people with post-graduate degrees. Who advertises that or even knows that about their neighborhood? In hindsight it planted a seed that would rapidly grow into more insecurity and jealousy when I decided not to attend law school.

I couldn't handle the wife role. I couldn't cook; the kitchen had always been taboo. Laundry and ironing were trial by error. Didn't know how to sew, and, quite frankly, didn't want to learn. I didn't do the Stepford gig well at all, but not for lack of trying.

However, I could decorate the house and keep it orderly and clean—too much so. A little obsessive, I realize now. One of my coping behaviors. My husband said I did it for me, not us, and there may have been some truth in that. But I thought that was the way a house was kept. Beautiful and impeccable. Inviting, warm, and cozy, just like my mother kept hers. Neil Diamond echoing throughout. I thought I had found my purpose. However, my jealousy and hunger for acceptance kept nagging at me. Relentless.

For me it had been love at first sight, with his contagious laugh and my rose-colored glasses. He was smart and funny. Compassionate and kind. An amazing father at this time, which charmed me a great deal. All of this fed my jealousy and shook my security. I never knew or understood where these feelings came from. During our first year of dating we had taken breaks from one another, and it wasn't until much later that I found out he had been sleeping with other women—many women—during those breaks, while I thought he was pondering our fate.

I had an ideal of marriage, the way my mom and dad loved one another. I had a father who respected and loved his wife more than anything. Never heard him say a negative word about her, and he reprimanded my brother and me for any modicum of disrespect. My dad was an honorable man with true devotion, evidenced over and over again.

That ideal was shattered by my husband's lack of understanding of who I was. Soon blaming me for my disease. A disease, not a choice.

He knew I had been committed to the psych ward at 16. He witnessed my eating behaviors while we were dating. He later argued that he didn't know about my illness until later on. In fact, I was asked by my divorce lawyer if I had disclosed my eating disorder to my ex prior to marrying him, because that would have been a deal breaker. Wow. Character and integrity nowhere to be found.

As time went by my jealousy waned and I had to get over being "the second wife." We found common ground in the love we shared for his little boy.

But my illness hadn't disappeared with my

marriage vows. There was no empathy. No acceptance and understanding from my husband. Even worse, he thought he understood. In fact, I don't remember anything that he thought he didn't know. Not me, though. He didn't know me at all. I remember him yelling at me during one of our early arguments that he was a good catch because, after all, he was a lawyer. Who says that to his wife?

Even now when I look back, I remember the hurt and the shame that coursed through me. His misunderstanding of our vows. My disappointment as those vows disappeared. Didn't they mean anything to him?

I became desperate. Unrelenting pain so deep I couldn't escape. So deep in my heart as it ached every moment—no break or relief. And I wasn't seeking help. The thought of doing so was dreadful. Scared out of my mind to do so, as I remembered Dr. Doom.

As my anxiety and eating disorder became unmanageable, so did my ability to do the simplest of things. I couldn't handle having food in the house. I couldn't eat in front of my husband. And when I did, I lost control. How awful for my young stepson, as I look back with regret. Couldn't leave my house often and soon not at all. Couldn't fake it when needed. Couldn't work and contribute as expected. Couldn't explain my pain. On the darkest of days I would lay on my couch with the shades drawn, unable to have a conversation. Ignored, when not yelled at and blamed for what I was doing to him. No compassion to be found. It was all about *him*.

Met with anger and denigration by my husband, who had no idea but thought he did. I remember him stating, in front of our divorce lawyers, that he knew better than anyone about eating disorders because he lived with me. "Not according to the professionals," my lawyer told him. This silenced his arrogance, at least for the moment.

I did feel loved and cared about by him for a while—a short while, before I got sick. I've looked at the wedding pictures and wondered what it would have been like had I not spiraled into darkness. Or if he had supported me throughout that time. I don't think I would have ever been what he wanted. Always selfish. Putting himself first. What was in it for him?

I didn't know what it was like to grow up on a farm in a small town. He told me he always dreamed of being a lawyer downtown and he worked very hard to get there. He wanted to be a judge and set himself up well for that appointment. Soon came the robe. He never mentioned me in his acceptance speech—not a word. Honorable?

When I went to events or retreats with members of his trade, I was mostly ignored or a cause of embarrassment when I could no longer hide my illness. Maybe it was a good thing being banished from such soirées.

Soon my illness was affecting his social rock climbing. During one of my ER visits, again very sick, he lamented in front of me and my friend how he was missing a judge's dinner. "*This always happens*," he said with anger. While I was fighting for my life, he left me with my friend so he wouldn't miss his dinner. For real? Again, I ask: *honorable?*

By this time he was leaving every weekend for the cabin we couldn't afford, whether I was in a bad spot or not. Fishing, camping, and a three-hour drive weren't my thing. Were never my thing. This should have been no surprise, as that was pretty clear from the get go. I enjoyed good company, Neil Diamond, and a nice place to hang my hat. I loved a roaring fire in the comfort of my living room, not in the woods.

Ongoing criticism and disrespect became the norm. Words that couldn't be taken back, that haunted me long after our divorce. What happened to the man who filled my heart?

My illness was merely a liability ruining his dreams while I was dying inside. Didn't he see that? Didn't he care? I was so sick—could anybody hear me? I was fighting for my life. For the happiness I deserved. Again, a lost cause.

I was told by many that I couldn't get better if I stayed in my marriage. The atmosphere was too caustic. The people who told me to leave were right, and yet I took my vows seriously—in sickness and health. For better and for worse. Until death do us part.

But I did see a therapist, a wise one at that. He referred me to an eating disorders program at a local hospital. No way—I wasn't going to do that again! My therapist ended up connecting me to a psychiatrist. I'll call him "Hawkeye" as we go forward (the doctor from the TV series M*A*S*H*). He knew eating disorders. He was the one who would ultimately save my life with his patience, compassion, and belief that I wasn't a lost cause.

Money was a big deal to my ex-husband. I didn't fully realize this until he chastised me for not being able to work. I received an ultimatum—get more help or we're done. I heeded his warning and went for an evaluation at the local hospital. They said to pack a bag, because if I was medically compromised I would be admitted right away, which is what happened as it turned out. My ex-husband was relieved I was getting appropriate care. I was back in a hospital, which terrified me—for good reason.

Again, the program's focus was to have me eat consistently and gain weight. Stabilization. I was mortified at the prospect. My husband feigned support when I followed the rules. But, much to his dismay, I needed more than a few weeks to unravel this dangerous disease, the fears that had consumed me, haunted me, for so many years. I didn't realize this at the time and promptly cut my stay short at the hospital. Only a handful of days left, I thought. What could happen in a few days, other than saddling me with a few more pounds? That was my rationalization.

The very day I was discharged from the hospital my husband took me to lunch at a restaurant, followed by a trip to the grocery store. *What?!?* That would be like taking a discharged heroin addict to the local drug spot. Patients are told specifically to take it slow when they're discharged from an ED program. More evidence of his lack of understanding and inability to listen. I was stabilized, not cured.

My roommate at the hospital had told me about a residential treatment center for ED, which I'll call Fantasy Island. It sounded beautiful, serene, and healing, with a small number of patients, only ten beds. I did my homework. Their promotional materials and website advertised their expertise in treating anorexia and bulimia, in solving the hardest cases. When I visited, the grounds were beautiful and everyone had a TV in their rooms. A gazebo for privacy and reflection. Even a pool to boot. A beautiful, tranquil location that took a holistic approach to the healing process. Far less intimidating than the confining, sterile, and cold hospital from years ago. I decided the program was for me and waited for an opening.

I looked fine now (apparently) with some weight restored, but I wasn't in recovery. For years I had looked healthy when I was seriously ill, as is common with eating disorders. I knew deep down that it would take more than a few weeks and a few pounds.

I wasn't back home for more than a few days when I was confronted about how we were going to pay for property taxes. For real? I didn't know how to eat dinner without panic, let alone enter the work world.

It wasn't long before my symptoms were back at full strength. And so was our dysfunctional relationship dynamic.

Why are you doing this? Why are you hurting me? You have a choice! You're not even trying!

Who would choose such misery? More ignorance at its best!

Angry from pain and darkness. Fed up as I lay paralyzed. Desperate for understanding. It seemed Fantasy Island was my only hope. In July 2007, after eight years of marriage, I arrived there for treatment.

Chapter Five

Enveloped in Madness

I arrived at Fantasy Island with trepidation, as my anorexia was in overdrive. I walked up the cobblestone walkway to be greeted by their head nurse. She was welcoming and kind, trying to make me feel at home. Her kindness and support beyond measure never wavered during my storm.

After searching my suitcase for contraband, like food or diet pills, they showed me to my room. A TV and bathroom. Pleased with the privacy, where I isolated in silence. Soon my room was locked during the day, forcing me into community areas that were intimidating and awkward as I tried to fit in. They wanted no malingerers hiding in their rooms. I was forced into the group schedule—art therapy, trauma groups, attachment groups, body image groups, guided imagery and movement groups. My coping mechanism was neatness and cleanliness, seeking control for the uncontrollable. In the middle of the night I would obsessively clean the common areas, which were a mess.

I was introduced to my therapist, who I would meet four times a week, instantly thinking she could help me. I would also meet once a week with the psychiatrist and dietician. The psychiatrist increased my medications dramatically, in power and number, the first time I met with him, which I thought was odd. Still, I trusted him. He said they would help with my underlying issues and reduce my anxiety about gaining weight. I was desperate for relief and dove in. Ironically, the side effect of many of these meds, which was never discussed, was either weight gain or extreme hunger.

After seeing my therapist for a handful of sessions she went on vacation, and in her absence I got to see Mr. Roarke, who had founded the center with either his wife or ex-wife—the story seemed to change like the weather. He wore loose white pants, a flowing white shirt to mid-thigh. Long gray hair. Larger than life, like a prophet, almost. A prophet I was desperate to believe in.

He ran the Island and there was no problem he couldn't fix. He was the one who could identify multiple personality disorders. He had treated over four thousand people who suffered from repressed memories. He had mastered what others couldn't identify, he told me more than once. I felt lucky he had become my primary therapist.

Mr. Roarke's office was one of kind, a bad museum of sorts. Shelves with countless books that were hard to ignore. He allowed me to clean his office on more than one occasion. This was his oasis and soon it was mine too.

He took a special interest in me. He said he could save my life and no one else could. He knew the answers to eating disorders that were as bad as mine. They weren't caused by normal stressors or triggers. I had deep-seated issues that I didn't know about and we had to get to the bottom of them. He was the best, I thought.

Roarke said to me, "We have to do hypnosis because I'm convinced that the cause is repressed memories." Again, this theory cropped up in my life. But now I wanted to believe it, had to believe it, because nothing else had ever worked.

I sat in the gazebo overlooking the grounds as I pondered my fate. I was enamored by his showman's façade, the mad scientist type. Had Dr. Doom been on to something so many years before? Was he not as skilled as Mr. Roarke in finding the real source of my illness? Maybe I had been abused, but by someone other than my dad. Would hypnosis get to the bottom of it? The Great Mr. Roarke seemed masterful. In a league of his own. He told me of countless cases that he alone had solved.

He was the self-proclaimed best. I now put all my trust in him.

My battles with food continued. If I didn't finish my plate in the allotted time frame, they gave me a supplement but I couldn't drink the dreadful stuff. I failed again and again. Soon came the feeding tube, which I carried around with me during the day. It was attached to my nose and my backpack contained the bag of calories. Some of the younger patients, who reveled in their medical complications, wore the feeding tube as a badge of honor. Not me, embarrassed with defeat. When I was caught tampering with the bag I had to carry mine around on an IV stand. My mind raced with ideas of how to drain it without notice.

I remained defiant about not eating and they started supplementing me with M&Ms and other fear foods—foods that terrified me because they were fattening. If I didn't eat my regular dinner, the punishment was candy. The outer limits! Not to mention unethical! My med list grew and grew, nearing twenty rather quickly. My days became murky and over-medicated—it was obvious to everyone. How could they work with me if I was a zombie? They knocked me out at night so thoroughly that I couldn't wake up to use the bathroom and slept in my filth.

After meals I wasn't able to go outside or to my room until my two-hour observation period was over. They were afraid that I would purge and over-exercise. The observation time was reduced as you earned more privileges. There was also a system that included four levels, with Level Four being the highest. I never progressed from Level One because of my non-compliance and my inability to eat consistently, or to know what my hunger cues were. My therapy rarely, if ever, was focused in a meaningful way on the specifics of my eating disorder, which got progressively worse.

I smuggled in Equal packets, a serious infraction. It didn't end there. The next was diet pills, discovered during their random room searches. How could I dare?

Yet I remained convinced only they could save me. I would otherwise die, Roarke told me several times.

The hypnosis, although it wasn't called that, was something I had never experienced before. I had never been in a situation where I would go out of consciousness into a deep trance I couldn't remember, and then have someone tell me what I had said when I returned to consciousness. Roarke described to me what happened when he reached my subconscious with the ease of his magic, but in my zombie state I rarely remembered our sessions. When I watched a videotape of a session, he did most of the talking, suggesting, and insinuating. He did ask the psychiatrist to scale back my meds a bit, as I often wasn't lucid enough to work with.

Mr. Roarke was a pro at manipulating me in conversation, leading me along and putting ideas in my head. "What I heard you saying is this," he would say, when I had said nothing. My body language told him I was repressing abuse.

Never once did I offer him a memory of any of this, but interpretation of my artwork assured him that abuse was in my past, he told me. Again, he was the only one skilled enough to uncover such severe trauma.

He sat next to me on his couch, interpreting one of my drawings. As abstract as it was, he drew his finger over it and said, "A cult. You are a member of a satanic cult." He assured me we could get through this. He had worked successfully on countless similar cases. He gave me reading materials on the subject. I believed he was telling me the truth.

Although he insisted I was a cult member, I failed to remember the details that he claimed hypnosis revealed. Terrifying accounts of my involvement in torture and murder. Fearsome rituals where I participated in sacrificing and eating children at each solstice. I was shattered to pieces by the horrors he recounted after he brought me out of my subconscious.

At one point Mr. Roarke had my friend R.T. convinced that he had to isolate me during the summer solstice and other times of cult danger. He took away my phone and computer during those times, or else my cult would contact me and I would run away to participate in satanism.

He put me on lockdown, and my family and husband had to use secret codes to contact me. Now I was totally isolated. Mr. Roarke said I was programmed to continuously return to the cult, to engage in a secret life of murder and sacrifice.

Maybe Roarke was on to something. It became plausible to me. Maybe I had been in a cult back home, engaging in horrific rituals, and didn't remember it. I had lived so much of my life inside my head, obsessed about food, weight, exercise, and my body, that it wouldn't be unusual if I had forgotten it all.

Roarke explained I had alters—about a dozen different personalities—to protect me from harm. I kept a list because I couldn't remember them all. There was a young child; there was Isabella, the seductress. Sometimes Roarke would get flirty with me and say, "Am I talking to Isabella?"

He told me that if I talked to anyone about the cult, even my husband, I would die by suicide because one of my multiple personalities would kill me for talking. He relayed these findings in a matter of fact way. I was diagnosed very quickly with DID or dissociative identity disorder, formally called multiple personality disorder (MPD), but essentially the same.

Insurance companies rarely covered MPD and were reluctant to cover DID. Roarke later told me that he couldn't call it DID on insurance claims. I'm not sure how it was documented. Nevertheless, my diagnosis was crystal clear, written in detail on my weekly contracts, signed by all members of their management team.

My friend R.T. would talk to my case worker from

my insurance company on a regular basis. When he mentioned treatment for DID, he was met with surprise. This was not mentioned in the notes she received from the Island. Many things were not communicated, such as the fact that I was getting much worse, not better. Confused, R.T. talked to Mr. Roarke about this error and requested he send an updated report explaining this omission. Roarke justified the omission by saying he could not provide this info because of HIPAA (the Health Insurance Portability and Accountability Act, which provides data privacy and security provisions for safeguarding medical information). Even though he had already violated my confidentiality by talking to R.T.! Roarke explained he would report what was needed to continue my insurance coverage.

My friend R.T. questioned Roarke about a statistic in one of the books Roarke had recommended, which stated that only 1.5% of psychiatrists made a diagnosis of DID. A very small percentage indeed. Roarke pushed back, claiming that most psychiatrists didn't know what to look for; he was the premier expert, the only one who could recognize the signs and call out my different personalities. Again, he had cured thousands of cases of DID.

During another conversation with R.T., Roarke

told him that through hypnosis he had discovered 22 separate identities in me and that he was the only therapist who had the expertise to communicate with them. He said that I would change personalities within ten seconds of his calling them out. Roarke had all 22 names memorized.

R.T. soon realized that all of the patients at Fantasy Island who had exceptionally good health insurance were being treated for DID—at least half the population of the center, which grew as time went on. During family weekends, these patients' families complained about being isolated from their children. My friend became suspicious of the validity of Mr. Roarke's diagnosis, especially when Roarke tried to convince him that all of his patients needed long term treatment—in excess of one year.

R.T. challenged Mr. Roarke's assertion that he had cured several thousand patients who suffered from DID. Roarke insisted he stood alone, having unparalleled skill in diagnosing the condition with speed and accuracy. R.T. confided his suspicions to me, but I was so brainwashed and stoned from medication that I couldn't process what he told me, let along remember it the next day.

We had weekly contracts outlining our assignments

and goals, with a med sheet that explained my woes. Over and over I was asked to name my alters—their personalities, their ages, and their functions, none of which I knew. Apparently only Mr. Roarke was in the know.

The dietician played the same game as Roarke, apparently having been instructed to talk to me about my alters in a "therapeutic" way: "Which alter am I talking to?" Totally inappropriate for a dietician. She was quite useless—I ended up gaining too much weight. Never learned how to portion my food or finish my plate. My assignments were focused on my alters, not on my struggle as I wrestled with food.

I got along with most of the on-line staff. Only a few would talk to you in normal ways, not about your various personalities.

The overnight specialist was wonderful and we had a special bond. She supported me through so much. She never received the respect she deserved from the higher ups but all the patients loved her. She helped me wash my sheets that were filled with my filth before anyone else awoke. When I was unable to sleep, she calmed me from my night terrors. She let me sleep in the common areas when my nightmares were overwhelming and I couldn't remain in my room. Whenever I began to drift away, she brought me back to the present moment. We would just talk and have a cigarette together. I'd help her clean up or make coffee.

I had a feeling she had an inkling about what was happening at Fantasy Island. When I would share some of my experiences, she looked uncomfortable. "I really don't know what to say," she remarked to me once, glancing away, "but I really need this job."

As I cowered in groups, trying to hide, Roarke talked for me to the other patients. Told the group how much he had helped me by finding my different personalities that were programmed by the cult. He seemed to be talking about someone else, but he said the story was mine.

I was horrified by the stories the other patients told in group, how they suffered from the unimaginable hell of sexual abuse, although most had no clear memories of such abuse before their arrival. Trauma "uncovered" by Fantasy Island. I was so overmedicated and under Roarke's spell that I didn't know what to believe.

Soon there was a DID group in the community, with at least 65% of the treatment center now diagnosed with the condition. Looking back, a big red flag, but I didn't see it. Roarke put me in touch with some past patients to provide me with "support and understanding." They spoke with me about the warning signs of cult activity. When they mentioned full moons and candles, which I love, it made me more worried, not less so.

I had no choice but to live in this ruined reality that was forced upon me. I longed for the days I had once known, before madness and medication had whispered their way into my very existence.

Mr. Roarke determined we needed to establish "an executive council" to keep me safe—three personalities that would control and console my other alters who were programmed to try to harm me. Together, we brainstormed: who were my strongest, most well-intentioned alters? Only the best could be on the executive council!

My behavior continued to be erratic and reckless. Beating a chair, shouting about my cult. Night terrors/ day terrors beyond my ability to cope. Insanity taunting me. "How do I heal?" I begged Mr. Roarke, who told me to leave it to him.

One night the staff left the med room unlocked by mistake. My escape from this madness was right there before me. I opened the second latch with a knife from dinner and raided the med room. Locked the door to my room, preparing for the end. Lined up the bottles of meds to hasten my demise. A handful of this and handful of that. A night nurse unlocked my bedroom door and saw the meds laid out on my bed. Had she not, I'd be dead.

I clung to her with all of my might. The next thing I remember I was in the hospital. Mr. Roarke was convinced that my suicide attempt showed that my executive council had failed miserably. We had to get control of my alters and Mr. Roarke had the answer. He shipped me off to a new treatment center. Owned by his brother, ironically.

This place was even farther from home, run down and sterile, more like a prison. Everyone struggled with disassociation. They had an open snack area and enough food for an army, throwing gasoline on my fire. Ravenous from my meds, I ate with a frenzy only noticed by me (or so I thought). I even ate my roommate's candy stash. A major boundary violation, met with her forgiveness. I was as out of control as I had ever been.

After seven months at Fantasy Island I returned home for a while, where I again tried to end my life, this time by hanging myself, but only ended up breaking my foot. They found fluid around my heart. More danger for me. Soon I could walk with my boot after much physical therapy and went back to Fantasy Island. Why, you ask. I still believed only Mr. Roarke could save me. Instilled in me by the one and only. *I would die without him*, he repeated.

One day I left the facility in a cab for a scheduled liposuction, because I was insanely freaked out by my body. The staff followed me to the doctor's, learning my whereabouts from the taxi I had taken. When I heard the Fantasy Island folks in the front office, the back door set me free. Evaded them for several hours (with a broken foot!).

Found down by a river. A psychotic break with no memory, a final break from reality. In the hospital's psych ward I was questioned and questioned about what happened to me. A doctor came in and said I was mentally ill. Contacted by the Island, I was not to be set free.

I remember calling Mr. Roarke, begging to return, and he said, "You left to fuck your uncle." The uncle who, in his mind and now mine, was the leader of my cult and who was having sex with me.

Appalled that I was trapped in a psych ward, my

father and a close relative drove for hours to rescue me and take me home.

Seven months of madness, and I was far worse when I returned home (other than weight gain, which was the marker of "success," a scary assumption). Consuming a gadzillion meds, hating my body more than ever. The last thing I wanted was anyone touching me, including my husband.

When he found out I broke into the medicine cabinet at Fantasy Island and took too many pills, it was over for him. He said no one could love me in my condition. That he had hung on for years even though he didn't think I would ever recover. I requested couples therapy; we had three sessions before he bowed out. Honorable? He was thinking of himself, as he always did. Once again, I was a lost cause.

He had visited Fantasy Island a handful of times. How could he have not noticed what was happening to me? I remember him saying, "The other girls got dolled up and looked good when their spouses came to visit." I was in hell and he wanted me to get dolled up? Being diagnosed with multiple personality disorder wasn't a red flag to him? Did he think that was my fault too? Not a red flag that I was drugged out of my mind? That I had a psychotic break and escaped Fantasy Island by the hair of my chinny chin chin? It was all apparently my fault. He even told me to find my own health insurance. His words so hurtful they seared like a knife. On the brink of insanity, I was left to fend for myself.

My heart broke when he told me how relieved he felt to take off his wedding ring. He moved out and five months later asked for a divorce. I was being eaten by a pack of wolves more fierce than any I had yet encountered.

I tried hard to convince my husband to come back, through kind notes and hopeful messages. I was delusional to think there was hope, since he had made up his mind long before and I was the last to know. The closer he was to dumping me, the nicer he became. Leaving me hopeful, but just part of his game, to ease my anger and hurt so we could avoid the lawyers and settle this on our own. Manipulated again while still so sick. How dare he? I'm guessing he had someone else already.

My dad saved me again by becoming my power of attorney through our bitter divorce. I had no doubt he would fiercely protect me, and that he did in the negotiations. I was grateful to know nothing about the process, which tells me it must have been awful. Thank you, dad. Before he stepped in, my ex wanted to be reimbursed for the items he paid for at our wedding. Oh, there's more. He wanted reimbursement for his travel expenses when he visited me at Fantasy Island. For real?

I had paid off his car and substantial credit card debt with my social security disability money, some of my safety net. Yet he accepted the money as though it had been deserved. I was 38 years old, disabled, vulnerable, and sick. Very sick. My heart had been stomped on enough.

Chapter Six

Into the Abyss

"Wherever you go, there you are."
–Jon Kabat-Zinn

No escaping my misery. At every turn, there I was, but I couldn't stand the skin I was in.

I was alone in my boat. Medicated and confused, not equipped for whitewater rafting.

After my husband moved out I received repeated messages from Mr. Roarke, telling me that I had left Fantasy Island "in the middle of surgery." *You'll die on your own*, he said. *You've got to come back here so I can help you. You left too soon and you need to finish.*

And, amazingly, I believed him, despite what my experience had been. I was on so much pain medication and prescription drugs that I couldn't even remember a good portion of what had gone on during my nine months with him, let alone analyze it rationally.

My divorce lawyer wanted to find out what

happened there and needed explanations from Mr. Roarke, who had convinced me that it was too dangerous to release my medical records or to talk about my psychotic break. Dangerous for whom?

I lay in my bed or on the couch in darkness for days on end. Drapes always drawn. Messages ignored. No light to be found. Days passed with not a word spoken or a voice heard. Starving for days, then eating out of control. Using Ipecac as a remedy, as I played with fire.

Deep in my darkness, my thoughts drifted from one tormented moment of my past to the next. Delusional feelings of bottomless guilt and inadequacy. Hopeless and alone, as Mr. Roarke had predicted. I had left in the middle of surgery and my fate was death. My boat was sinking rapidly, saddled with the weight of my past. I was rowing alone, sapping any energy I had left.

My sleep was filled with nightmares of ritual satanic cults, bloody, violent nightmares of babies being killed, a horror I had come to believe I had perpetrated. Night terrors, day terrors, unrelenting and fierce. I couldn't sleep in my bed; I had to sleep on the couch facing the front door. My speech was slow as I searched for words, when I was able to speak at all.

All alone with the black beast of depression, awful beyond words or sounds or images. No belief in the possibilities of life, let alone in the need to shower or get dressed. Ordinary tasks seemed monumental. I didn't want this life. I couldn't do it anymore. My boat and I alone, struggling to stay afloat.

Uh oh. A police officer, pounding on my door. *You have the right to remain silent.* He held a prescription before me and asked if it looked familiar. I was numb. He let me change before walking me to his car. I called no one, ashamed and distraught.

Several weeks before I had an appointment with a doctor I had been seeing since I was 15 years old, my OBGYN who I trusted for years (a huge feat for me). He taught me how to ski. Listened to me always. Sage advice constantly. He was my favorite, and yet I betrayed him. When he handed me my prescription, he had ripped two blank forms off his pad. I went back and forth and back again. Finally I forged a prescription for Valium with several refills but it lacked directions for use. The pharmacy called my doctor for clarification. The next call was to the police.

At the police station I was handcuffed until processed. Was this a bad dream? A wicked scene from a movie? Fingerprints, mug shot, and my weight (which I saw, an all-time high).

Was I really that heavy? I hadn't weighed myself since I returned home from Fantasy Island.

I spent the night locked in a room the size of my closet, with a toilet and bed. Stuck in my head, unable to sleep, overwhelmed by repulsion for myself and that hideous number I saw on the scale. I was arrested and in jail for a serious offense, and yet my mind went wild with that number, a number so foreign to me. *Wake up, Lisa! You're in jail!*

Morning soon came and the lieutenant insisted I sit down as I paced with worry, still obsessed about the number.

"Is your scale accurate?" I asked. "It just can't be right."

He looked at me, dumbfounded; the room thickened with silence as I awaited his words.

"How much pain are you in?" he asked me.

Now I was dumbfounded, not imagining this curve ball. Soon I was sobbing. "I'm in so much pain I don't know how to survive or even if I want to." He listened with compassion, not the reaction I anticipated, one I never thought I would meet from a police officer.

He told me my dad was downstairs to pick me up.

What?!? The distress on his face was inescapable as I trembled with shame. We walked to the car in silence; his disappointment left us searching for words. Then he spoke. "How could you do this? This is a felony. I can't help you with this, it's out of our hands."

I had betrayed my doctor, dad, and myself. It was a moral lesson I would never forget and never repeat. Yet still my overriding obsession was shrinking my weight at any cost.

My father called a lawyer he knew. Months passed as I awaited my fate. Then I went before a judge again. He was calm and controlled as he delivered my sentence for the forged prescription. I hardly heard what he said as I reverted back to being 16, when another judge had committed me. Fear and fury filled my head. But the judge was kind and understanding. I wasn't an evil person who committed a heinous crime. He concluded I needed treatment for my eating disorder, depression, and anxiety. Back to the Island, he ordered, along with a year on probation and periodic drug testing. I had no room for error.

Believe it or not, had the judge not ordered me back, I still believed that Mr. Rourke could save my life. If there's any measure of how ill I was, that was it.

As my boat floated adrift, I waited for an opening on Fantasy Island. Days went by without eating. The worse I got, the more I was convinced it was my fault. I couldn't self-medicate because of the drug testing. The number on the scale took over my every thought. Food—weight—shape. That was all.

My boat, barely afloat, drifted back to the Island, so serene and remote. I would die without his help, he said. Petrified this might be true, I surrendered.

On my return, I was devastated that Roarke wasn't my therapist. He had a new project and didn't have time to see me. I wept for days after he brushed me away, distraught, abandoned by the self-proclaimed healer, who had assured me he would help me as no else could. I had to "earn" any sessions with him, no longer his "flavor of the month." If I jumped through some hoops, if I admitted to being a Satanist, he said I could see him once a week. *Until then, talk to Tattoo.* And so I did.

My dad called every morning, leaving a message that he loved me, helping me stay grounded, from going completely insane.

Tattoo, my new therapist, was quite different, not in method but in temperament. He listened intently, although he believed in the same craziness as Mr.

Roarke. Respectful and kind. Even-tempered at the hardest of times. He checked in on the reality of what was on my mind—food, stressors—but his overall approach was the same. I was the victim of a satanic cult.

I was sure Mr. Roarke had briefed him, as Tattoo knew of the horror that tormented me. We dove into the darkness that Roarke had uncovered, working on "memories" that infected my mind. I was ready to do anything so I could see Roarke again. I thought he was my savior.

After one session with Tattoo I asked him if I could shower, because I felt so dirty from what we had talked about in session. When he declined, I walked in a daze to the pool and jumped in to cleanse myself. When I reentered the facility, Tattoo was talking to a staff person in the hallway; neither had any reaction to my soaking clothes.

I wasn't getting any better, so my insurance company finally put its foot down and set some limits. I was transferred to "step-down," where I had more personal freedom. The program allowed us to live in a house of our own and drive our cars. We had more free time but participated in most of the same groups. Afraid to be alone and not supervised by staff, I didn't see this program as a help. What if a cult member abducted me? No one in my condition should have been sent to that program. But Mr. Roarke gave me a tour of the house and sold it to me. No insurance coverage should have paid for it.

At one point the residential home didn't even have a bed for me. I was left to sleep on the floor or couch. Not even a cot or another alternative. Unbelievable.

I became increasingly unhinged. Because they cut back on my medication, sleeping was more frightful than ever before. Sometimes I threw my supplement at the staff. I wouldn't do assignments— i.e., explain how the summer solstice was celebrated in my cult—because I had no memory of what they wanted. I was cited for non-compliance and I ended up with the most non-compliance reports, giving them every opportunity to kick me out. Why didn't they? Many people were kicked out arbitrarily, for far fewer infractions than I had. Was it because my insurance, although cut back somewhat, kept paying?

I didn't learn anything in the new program, reverted back to my eating behaviors, still struggled with food.

Roarke became vindictive when I questioned him on things. He ridiculed me in front of the group, whether I was there or not. *Lisa isn't cooperating. She's a bad patient. Lisa wants to go back to her cult.*

We always had a group meeting at the beginning of each week where everyone checked in about how their past week went. Roarke now skipped calling on me. He cut me off if I tried to give feedback. He encouraged the other group members to criticize me and question my word, leaving me with no opportunity to explain or defend myself. Sometimes he applauded group members who confronted me.

Less medicated and more lucid now, I began to see through his game. He treated me as though his vendetta was personal, noticed by more people than just me. I was set up, shamed, and villainized. Good therapy? Do no harm? But no one questioned him. No one would dare. But now I was beginning to do so.

At the same time, my friend R.T. again shared his conversations with Mr. Roarke, creating increasing doubt in me. I had no idea Roarke had been telling R.T. I would never get better. HIPAA? Roarke followed no rules.

As I challenged him, Mr. Roarke reacted with rage. He had me detail all my life's wrongs to the group. What a bad person I was. How crazy I was acting. Was this therapeutic? Wasn't I supposed to be made better, not shamed and pushed to the limits of my sanity? Pure evil. Can you hear me?

Mr. Roarke was methodical and calculating as he manipulated my advocate at the insurance company. They would not cover DID or multiple personality disorder at this time. He came up with another name and the insurance coverage kept flowing. My contact and advocate at the insurance company was briefed weekly, I was told. She had doubts about my treatment but it wasn't her call. Later she was transferred to another position for pointing out to her superiors that something wasn't quite right at Fantasy Island.

When my insurance company finally put a deadline on my coverage, I was treated far differently than before. Received a lot less attention. Shunted aside. I became increasingly skeptical of the number of patients diagnosed with DID, of all the accusations of cult activity. When I departed for a fictitious divorce meeting in early December, I left all my things behind, drove home, and never returned. Fantasy Island bagged my possessions, and my friend R.T. picked them up several weeks later.

Part Three

Not a Lost Cause

Chapter Seven

Done Too Soon

"People are like stained-glass windows. They sparkle and shine when the sun is out, but when the darkness sets in, their true beauty is revealed only if there is a light from within."

–Elisabeth Kubler-Ross

I returned home from the Island in December 2009. For good. After $700,000 paid by my insurance company and gaining a bucket of weight, I was far worse than ever before. Severely depressed. My eating habits completely erratic. Horror filling my nights, when I could distinguish between night and day.

So many regrets over more lost time. I hid away from life, just wanted to be in total darkness, my drapes always shut. Not a light on, but always a roaring fire.

During this time I met a young woman who lived not far away. She had been on the Island with me and had experienced the same madness. As we met several times in my home and talked, she told me her story, unraveling her shock and repulsion. I was riveted by what she said. At Fantasy Island she had been warned to have no contact with me. Why?

She had taken copious notes during her time there and her account of her experience would slowly set me free. She told me what Mr. Roarke said about me behind my back after I left Fantasy Island. That I had left the Island to return to my cult. That was I was engaged in pornography, child sacrifices, and murder. That I was dangerous and to be avoided, or else she would be devoured by my cult. My friend's survival depended on staying far away from me.

Reading her journal stunned me. She provided me with an objective, first-hand view of what had happened to me. The details of what she experienced destroyed any last doubt in me. She too had been programmed. Implanted with false memories. Overmedicated. Diagnosed with DID. Lies so atrocious, how did I ever believe them? How could this have happened? Why didn't I see?

As my friend gently provided the truth, the façade of Fantasy Island totally unraveled. No evidence-based treatment, just reckless theories and convincing lies.

Still I received messages from Roarke, telling me not to leave the area or I would die. It was nearing the end of my year of probation and drug testing. Mysteriously, my probation officer received an anonymous phone call suggesting I should be drug tested one more time before they vacated my probation. It had to be Mr. Roarke, devious and cowardly, out to punish me. I passed the drug test and the charges were dropped. Much to his dismay, I imagine.

My home became a cocoon. I was living in darkness, quite literally, with just light from the TV. Again, the drapes remained drawn all day. Just the tick of the grandfather clock proved time was passing. No food in the house. On my rare trips outside I mastered pleasantries, as some encounters were unavoidable. Most people ignored me, my preference indeed.

I had only brief visits with mom, as my anxiety was too high to leave my cocoon for long. Messages from her went unanswered. I was unraveling. My visits with her became less frequent, as I tried to hide my despair.

My dad said, "You know what? You've got to visit your mom more because she's ill." And I would try, but I was simply not there like I should have been. I was avoiding everyone. Lost time with her I would deeply regret. Time I would never get back.

On my 40th birthday I sat alone in the darkness, ignoring my mom's plea for a celebration. Outrageous and unbelievable. How could I let this happen, missing memories we could have shared? How could I deny her our relationship once again? But I was caught in a tunnel of fear, trapped with my demons. No excuse. Just my reality. It was my last birthday I had with her.

At the end of 2010 my mom went into the hospital for an infection, but was positive and loving as always. Longing to see me. So excited by my visits. Pleading with me to find out how long she had to stay in, anxious with an anticipation I knew all too well. Hospitals were awful.

When I asked the doctor, he replied, "Well, she's got about six months."

I was asking how long she would be in the hospital. I believed she was going to live for many years to come. Numb with disbelief, my heart dropped to the floor, shattered. I asked him what he meant and he was very clear. He mentioned hospice care. I pleaded for another option, for more time. Was he sure about his prognosis? How could he know this? What could we do?

From that moment I never left her side. This doctor was wonderful, as he helped guide me through this terrifying reality I had never imagined.

Her multiple sclerosis made her immobile and in need of abundant care. It was devastating to watch the disease steal her mobility and independence. Her wish was to remain at home, no hospitals anymore. The doctor was compassionate and thorough, and agreed to come to her home and make her as comfortable as possible. My brother held on to moments of hope as she rebounded and seemed to be more present. My heart ached as his eyes reflected this hope. But she was passing through the stages of dying.

"Were the doctors wrong?" my brother asked with uncertainty. Breaking my heart with his wish for more time. He had taken care of my mom with love and compassion, year after year. With unwavering dedication. Something I admire and revere. But I wasn't even half-way there. I can't just blame my illness. I was selfish and in denial. I wince as I think of the impact my absence had on her. All she wanted was my company and my love. How could I fail her simple wishes?

I fought my demons, trying to keep them at bay. Buried deep for a while, but bubbling again to the surface no matter how hard I fought them. I had only six months to mend and repair my relationship with my mom. Through the grace of God, I found my strength and devotion. Although I never thought I could endure it, with the help of my aunt, my pillar and partner without hesitation, we were with her nearly round the clock. My aunt was miraculous. Words cannot describe. We worked as a unit, finding our way each day with my dad and brother, who always were there. Always! True devotion. Again, can't be put into words. I was finally back with my family, finding strength and vigor I had never imagined, that had been foreign to me for so incredibly long. I didn't want to miss a minute with mom. No time to spare. My family embraced me with their unconditional love, despite my past failures and unforgivable absence. My brother was always an amazing young man. Beyond measure. A hero.

Mom was the boss. All on her terms—she told us she wanted to die at home with dignity, courage, and grace. She was able to live in the moment. What a remarkable gift. She was a fighter and tried every remedy she could. At times she lit up and I would forget about her dreadful fight with MS, one she had tackled with all her might. So brave and selfless.

A fateful day arrived when my dad called and said to come over right away. She was hallucinating and wouldn't let anyone in the room but my dad and step-grandmother. She shouted, "Don't come in! Or you'll be taken away with me!" As time passed and she became lucid again, I remember her crying, not knowing what to expect: "I always knew what was next and now I just don't know." Death was a mystery. My dad and I had no answers but shared her tears.

I always thought crying meant I was out of control. But I sobbed and shook uncontrollably with the reality that we were losing her. She called a meeting with my brother, my dad, and me, a St. Patrick's Day I will never forget. She sensed it was time and told us how proud she was of us. Proud of me? After all I had put her through with my illness? Unimaginable. Asked us to take care of each other. I will never let my boys down, I vowed.

But we were blessed with a few more months. When she was near the end and I was apologizing for my absence and selfishness, she stopped me and said, "Let's put that behind us and enjoy the time I have left." She was always forgiving but I could not forgive myself. She eased my mind of my many regrets. We were able to say anything and everything that was on our minds, with laughter and tears. She told me to carry on, with my dad and brother, the holiday traditions that she loved so well. I was so grateful I had this time to make peace with her. She helped put my heart back together and taught me how to love again. A tremendous gift she gave so effortlessly. Even throughout her suffering, her love for all remained strong, unwavering.

She died soon after, surrounded by our family and close friends. Holding her hand when she left this world was extraordinary and powerful beyond words. Time didn't stop. The sun kept beaming and I stared at the yard, the plush green grass, her favorite lilac bushes. Did the world know of this loss, that my world had changed forever?

I thought we were robbed. She was only 63. People tried to comfort us or make sense of her death. I would often hear, "Well, at least she's not suffering anymore." Perhaps they were right, but it offered little comfort.

She was an ER nurse before I was born; then she reached her calling as a full-time mom. She was a talented cook and baked like a pro. We had the best Halloween costumes of anyone we knew. She could paint and design—any home project she tackled with pleasure. She was the Easter Bunny on Easter, Santa on Christmas. The master of ceremonies at birthday parties. She had a gift closet and had a present for everyone who came through her doors. She had more fun giving than receiving.

She was a voracious reader. Our trips to the library and bookstores are cherished memories. The smell of new books. Using my imagination more than television allowed. She always cheered me on unconditionally. Dance recitals. Band concerts. Piano lessons. Swimming lessons. Telling me I could do anything I put my mind to.

When we came home from our annual shopping trips before my birthday and Christmas, we couldn't wait to tell dad how much we saved. He'd respond with a smirk, "But how much did you spend?" Our Sunday drives were delightful, with her singing and all. But I loved her birthday the best, on New Year's

Eve. We went to a fancy restaurant and she would splurge on a grasshopper she allowed us to taste. She was a lady. One of a kind.

Where did my self-hatred and self-doubt come from, having been so loved?

Now you understand
Just why my head's not bowed.
I don't shout or jump about
Or have to talk real loud.
When you see me passing,
It ought to make you proud.
I say,
It's in the click of my heels,
The bend of my hair,
The palm of my hand,
The need for my care.
'Cause I'm a woman
Phenomenally.
Phenomenal woman,
That's me.
–Maya Angelou

That's my mom. Yes indeed.

Chapter Eight

A Righteous Anger

I sat on the hearth, staring into the fireplace. Mesmerized by the dancing flames and the crackle of the wood. Although it was July, I needed the comfort of a fire. I could tolerate one in the summer heat because my anorexia always left me cold. The hearth was my place of calm and safety, even in my worst moments. My always comforting perch.

My mind was going very fast, too fast. Tormenting me with a dreary litany of my inadequacies and shortcomings in character. It was exhausting, overwhelming. The numbing voice I had heard all my life. The reminder I was a lost cause, heard from many.

I felt as though I had lost everything, that anorexia and its madness had finally defeated me. My soul was broken beyond repair, spiraling into the abyss. If I couldn't feel, if I couldn't move, if I couldn't think, and if I couldn't care, then what conceivable point was there in living?

My marriage, my home, and any semblance of a professional life were all gone, and now my mind as well. I had felt intolerably overweight ever since I left the Island. I was so obsessed and embarrassed about it that I rarely left the house. For the previous two years I had been pretty much a recluse, paralyzed by my body image and major depression. It seemed all my fears were being realized.

I don't really know how I spent my time. I was simply lost in my thoughts, day in and day out, week in and week out. There was no reprieve from my torment, aside from the last six months of my mother's life when I felt strong and my eating disorder was on the back burner and everything was focused on her. But now, after her passing, I was just lost in my madness.

The nights were agonizing for me; I was petrified to go to sleep. Terrible nightmares about the unspeakable atrocities I experienced on the Island. Tried to sleep during the day with no luck. Watched TV for hours on end, without being able to tell you what I had seen. Showering was beyond my capacity. Even undressing exhausted me, so I often slept in the same clothes for days. Not new for me.

The fire roared on, and so did my desperation. Darkness unrelenting. More afraid to live than to die.

Even wonderful Hawkeye couldn't help me. I hid my self-destructive feelings from him in our therapy sessions.

Holding tight to my bottle of Ativan, I tried to determine how many would calm me down. I really needed my mom. She had been gone for exactly one year now. My heart just hurt beyond anything I ever felt. I needed her to tell me it was going to be okay. I needed to see the love and delight in her eyes.

Emptied the bottle of pills into my palm and held them for a moment. Could I do this? Two big gulps later I had, hoping to fall asleep and not wake up, convinced my family and friends would be better off without me. Would they say at least she's not suffering anymore?

Within moments of swallowing the pills I became frightened of the unknown. I needed to talk to someone while I waited for sleep to envelop me. A crisis line, I thought, as time ticked by. I could be anonymous and hear a comforting voice as my world faded to black. I made the call. When the line was answered, I told him that I didn't know how to deal with the next ten minutes or so.

I remember sitting on the floor as he kept asking me questions. I was getting confused; there was no comfort to be found. Why couldn't he just help me through the next few minutes? Drowsiness settled in. I hung up.

Made my way to the couch to lay down when the front door rattled from fierce pounding and pounding. The police. My call had not been anonymous. *That's bullshit*, I thought.

"Open the door or we will!" More pounding. Policemen all over, as I was fading away. I was pretty obstinate through my haze. Wouldn't tell them what I took. I stumbled to the hearth. One kind policeman sat with me and said, with compassion, "Come on…" No anger or judgement. He was trying to save my life. I told him what I took, how much, and when. They rushed me out immediately. Oh my god, what had I done? Waning to darkness—numb.

M y next memory was waking up in the hospital. Struggling to adjust to my surroundings, to realize where I was. Almost two days had passed. The nurse was intent on waking me, as the shrink had arrived.

The surroundings were familiar and the game was

the same. No remedy for my deep despair. Get me out of here pronto. But I had no choice other than to live in a broken world forced upon me. Madness, my mind, my life.

I would be kept under observation for 72 hours, until my condition was stabilized. The notorious "72-hour hold" that had been used for almost thirty years when they didn't know how else to help me. But something was different about this one.

I was foggy and confused as the shrink talked to me about a conversation we apparently had had the day before, of which I remembered nothing. In a bewildered tone, he said, "If your weight troubles you, then do something about it. Lose a little weight." He added, "We're not going to have this conversation again because it's just not worth it."

An unfamiliar feeling surged through me. I was angry at someone other than myself, for perhaps the very first time. A light bulb turned on, almost too bright to see. *Just "do something" about anorexia? Just lose some weight? Choose not to have an illness that had hijacked my mind? Being lectured like a child after a suicide attempt?*

How dare he! I had finally had enough. Misunderstood since I was 12 years old. Thirty years later, in 2012, I was still being told that anorexia was simply a matter of choice!

It had been a few years since I had been hospitalized. For me, that was a long stretch, and I thought I would never be back. I was furious now. Angry about not being listened to, about being grievously misunderstood once again.

I couldn't get the shrink's words out of my head—his suggestion that I had a lack of volition! Just lose some weight and your nightmares will soon fade! Was it a lack of volition that had ruled my life for the last thirty years? My choice to be committed to a psych ward at age 16, where I spent an entire year of high school? My choice to endure a failed marriage, suicide attempts, and a depression so fierce that I couldn't leave the house?

I kept obsessing over his ridiculous words. But the hopelessness and searing pain continued to morph into anger. I had never felt this kind of anger before. At myself, yes, and toward undeserving others, but never toward my "treatment." That anger was a godsend—it started me on the path to begin to challenge my endless shame.

I realized it wasn't a question of the hospital having a punitive feeling; rather, it *was* punitive, plain and simple. Blamed for my illness. Not treated as a patient who desperately needed help. Enmity towards me and my eating disorder. In their eyes the problem was created by me and was mine alone to solve.

I had thought I was damaged beyond repair. But there was a light of hope within me, just a hint but strong enough, a hope fueled by my anger. A choice? Damn you all!

After the 72 hours expired, my brother picked me up and took me home. I'll never forget the look on his face. He was very uncomfortable as we tried to rush through the hospital doors.

"Why didn't you tell us you needed help?" he asked. "Why don't you talk to us? Why don't you call us? What were you thinking?"

"I wasn't," I replied.

When I finally left the hospital, I knew a couple of things. My suicide attempt had been impulsive. If I hadn't succeeded, I had to find a way to take care of myself and to fight for recovery. And the second was to fight for an understanding of eating disorders. I had endless questions about my journey through hell and now I had to find the answers. I wanted to help make change, but I didn't understand how to do that because I didn't yet understand myself and what I had been through.

My father's house was very empty without my mother there, but at least I was not alone as he cared for me, telling me he couldn't bear to lose me. I was surrounded by memories of mom as I drifted off. Whenever I was sick as a child, she comforted me in a way that no one could ever match. Stroking my hair, helping me to forget any sadness with each gentle brush of her hand. If I closed my eyes tight enough I could feel it. The warmth in my heart that would never leave. I would have given anything and everything to have had her with me at that moment. Every moment.

I had to stop letting life just happen to me. I had to fight my demons toe to toe, armed with knowledge and the protection of the truth on my side. I had to do this if I were to live, to save myself from from the darkness that had me paralyzed for years.

Nevertheless, I went off the radar again, off the grid. I couldn't leave my house, couldn't pick up the phone. However, I soon tried, despite my familiar unrelenting anxiety, to reconnect with my friends and my family. Met with excitement that I was reaching out. Hawkeye was right—I couldn't do this alone. I hung on to his optimism for dear life. With great patience, having to repeat and repeat himself, until I entertained a slight possibility of hope.

I was terribly afraid Hawkeye would abandon me. I explained to him the desperation that led to my attempt and shared what the shrink from the hospital had said. I even asked the shrink to call Hawkeye and leave a detailed message about me on his phone. I was in Hawkeye's office when he called and together we listened to the message. The shrink talked about how psychologists in Europe thought eating disorders were the result of schizophrenia. He repeated that I lacked volition and could simply lose weight if I wanted to. He asked Hawkeye to call him back, but of course he didn't bother. Why respond to that bullshit?

My friend, the young woman who had also been at Fantasy Island, had enough fight even for me. She walked me through the maze of my perceived defeat. Smart beyond her years and cunning as could be. She would lead me to resources to help me understand. Experts and articles she shared with me—about phony repressed memories and brainwashing and DID. I soon understood how I had been driven to insanity. Calculated indeed. Mr. Roarke created a false identity for many, not just me. I read and I read the articles with awe, as if they were talking to me. I wasn't an idiot or crazy as they had wanted me to believe.

I requested all my medical records, dating back to Dr. Doom, to piece together this puzzle called me. All but the Island's records were forthcoming. I was stunned as I read Dr. Doom's notes about me so many years later, as an adult. "Denial" and "coerced" and "pressured" were just a few of his comments in my records. Being labelled in denial I could understand. But coerced and pressured? It was only three decades later that I understood he was admitting, in black and white, that he used those tactics on 15-year-old me: "I did coerce her to entertain the possibility of A, B, or C happening…" Recklessness beyond measure.

Months went by as I waited for my records from Fantasy Island. When they finally arrived, I was shocked again. Dr. Roarke wrote in his notes that he was scared of me—I was the "black widow" who had made two men commit suicide. Outrageous comments that should never come from a medical professional. His notes were also out of order about things that had happened in my life and during my stay. Nothing matched my weekly contracts that were signed by the entire treatment team. It was obvious that Roarke had tampered with his notes, twisting around things I had said to him and had not said.

I had naively believed in the power of hypnosis to break the barrier that supposedly separated me from unconscious repressed memory. It would lead to a big breakthrough. A complete illusion. Probing for material that didn't exist. But Mr. Roarke kept digging and digging. There had to be more, he thought, although I had no pre-therapy memories of satanic abuse. He "diagnosed" this deep-seated cause through artwork and my ED symptoms. The reality he sold was created in therapy, manufactured by a self-proclaimed expert who claimed expertise like no other. I kicked myself for not having had the strength or wisdom to have seen through the charade much earlier.

Dr. Roarke was a liar along with those who followed his lead. Confirmed in black and white, set in ink. This knowledge helped me as I tried to break free. But why had he done this? Money? Power? Just plain evil? I will never know the motivations and had to learn not to care. I purged my home of all their poison. I threw out anything from the Island or that reminded me of it. It was a huge relief to do so. If only

I could have removed the poison that still ran through my veins.

I binged on Neil Diamond music that soon got me off the couch, as I danced over and over and over. He was singing my song. This helped me stand on both feet, to fight my trouncing and take back my reality.

Chapter Nine
Pretty Amazing Grace

I had a lot of unraveling to do. Again, a critical time. I saw Hawkeye only sporadically when I was between visits to the Island because I was in a self-medicating haze most of the time. I gave him just the briefest overview of what happened to me, far too embarrassed to tell him about the hell I survived. I was afraid that if I told him, he would think I was a lost cause and he would abandon me.

Hawkeye was a scientist and professor. I asked him over and over if I had DID and he said no, absolutely not. Relief and understanding that he—the best— didn't think so. My DID had been diagnosed within weeks of arriving on the Island; now I found out that it usually takes *nearly seven years* to diagnose (if, in fact, it exists at all; it's in the DSM, but I remain skeptical).

Hawkeye understood my language or lack thereof. He understood eating disorders. He was the best of the best. He believed in evidence-based care, which I had never heard of until I left Fantasy Island. He saved my life. I would not have survived had he given up.

He repeated and repeated that there was hope. That I could recover, that my efforts, thoughts, intentions, and beliefs needed to change and could change. Repeated until it began to sink in. Reminded me more times than I could count what my past behaviors had resulted in—a dead end of misery. Asked me to have compassion for myself. Would I judge my friends as harshly as I judged myself if they had had my experiences? Provided me with cold hard facts, not theories and supposition and reckless diagnoses.

His patience should be bottled and sold. He promised to see me when I was 70 if need be. Assuaging my insecurity, that he'd give up or leave, which had been a huge fear. He didn't treat me as irrevocably damaged. How he put up with me and believed in me surprises me to this day.

I deserved Hawkeye's great care, considering my past "therapy." I had to learn to manage my chronic major depression, which was also a disease, period. I needed to manage my panic and anxiety—also a disease, period. I learned to manage through skills and pills. Hawkeye carefully found a medicine regime for me, including an antidepressant, an antipsychotic to help boost my antidepressant, and an antianxiety med. I was determined to manage without medication and tried to do so not just once, but four times. Learning the same lesson each time, as I quickly spiraled down into a paralyzing depression. Brutal. Okay, okay, I would take my medicine and wouldn't be ashamed to take it. To dismiss mental illness as a weakness that you can white knuckle through is foolish at best, deadly at worst.

I had lived in my head forever—food, weight, and body image consumed all my thoughts. When I could even think, that is. Now I had finally found the right care, evidence-based care—the right medication, cognitive therapy, and exposure therapy to cure my agoraphobia. My assignment was to leave the house once a week—me, who didn't leave my house for weeks. No way, I thought, but I trusted Hawkeye and fiercely tried.

I realized how lucky I was that Hawkeye felt I was worth the investment, that I wasn't a lost cause. I had a huge mountain to climb. He helped me see the light and believe in the possibility of recovery. He had no doubt. He was the most patient, optimistic person I have ever known.

Hawkeye helped me navigate through my divorce

and my mother's death. He helped me accept my diagnoses and cope through the darkest of days. He helped me learn how to feel and forgive, to accept and cope. I didn't know who I was, but he helped me begin to put my puzzle back together. The puzzle of me.

We could have wasted more time pointing fingers at why I was so sick and looking for huge demons that just were not there. I had a disease. Period. He added PTSD to my daunting list—diagnosed for the first time, after nightmares about the Island kept me awake all night. Hawkeye also told me that 50% to 80% of my illness was determined by genetics. WOW! This news helped chip away at my self-hate and humiliation.

Hawkeye pushed me to my limits but only as far as he believed I could go. Building my coping skills was quite difficult. Proper nutrition and moderate exercise were and remain my biggest challenge. Medication side effects included weight gain; I wrestled with this but learned the hard way what would happen if I didn't take my meds. I never thought I could manage or avoid my panic attacks. *Breathe, Lisa, breathe*, I told myself, *breathe in for two and out for two* whenever my heart felt it would beat through my chest, believing I was going to die.

But I got up and tried every day. My good days grew through the darkness. I tried to start each day with gratitude, then Neil Diamond. My moods began to lift. Hawkeye never gave up. My recovery process was not linear, but I was blessed with pretty amazing grace. It's never too late.

I had not looked in a mirror since I gained so much weight. When I finally looked, I didn't recognize who I saw staring back at me. Aged and worn down, although I felt quite a bit younger. Young at heart, I guess. Forever, I hope.

I realized I had been tyrannized by a notion of happiness. An idea of what would bring me peace but that instead made me suffer. If only I could lose five more pounds. If only I had a different body. If only I had a different past. Always seeking the approval of others. I thought happiness meant being married and having a career and being an integral part of my community. But when I had all those conditions in place, I had no internal happiness, no ability to appreciate the small things.

Preoccupied with worries and my suffering, obsessed with mourning and regretting my past and fearing the future, I was continuously missing out on the present. Missing out on life. Postponing being alive.

My dad has an amazing ability to take one day at a time. "We'll cross that bridge when we come to it," he likes to say. But I fear my bridges will explode. What an awful way to live.

I had a desperate desire to let go of my false ideas. I had to train myself to live in the present moment. Each hour is precious. A gift.

I knew I was afraid to look inside, that I had a lot of internal suffering and conflict I wanted desperately to avoid. I had escaped in the past by turning on the television, by self-medicating, by running away from myself as fast as I could.

But when I ran away, I never escaped. I had only one choice—to work hard, painfully hard, in therapy with Hawkeye. I continued to push against limits that had seemed unattainable time after time. I started to get in touch with the courage to contemplate my response to whatever crises that came my way, rather than always reacting in the same patterns of the past. But most of all, to live in the present. It was living in the past and future that had almost destroyed me. Letting go of that illusion is a practice and an art, one that I had begun to entertain.

Part Four

A Call to Action

Chapter Ten
Hypnosis, Hoaxes, and Hysteria

In the 1980s, a mass hysteria swept our country. It began in 1983 when the operators of the McMartin daycare center near Los Angeles were charged with raping and molesting dozens of small children. Many of the allegations were outrageous—teachers chopping up animals, clubbing horses to death with baseball bats, ritually sacrificing babies, and making children drink blood and eat feces. Teachers reportedly dressed up as witches and flew through the air. All of this apparently took place without notice by parents, neighbors, and authorities. The trial that resulted was the longest and costliest in American history. It unleashed a nationwide panic about child abuse and ritual satanism in our daycare centers and schools.

The McMartin daycare center wasn't the only source of this panic. A teacher at a daycare center in Maplewood, N.J. was convicted in 1988 of sexually abusing children. Six years later, her conviction was overturned. Operators of a daycare center in Edenton, N.C. were accused of raping and sodomizing young children; there were allegations of babies being murdered and thrown in with sharks. Defendants were found guilty, but their convictions were also eventually overturned.

In the McMartin case, no convictions were obtained after six years of criminal trials and all charges were dropped in 1990. There had been no sacrifices of babies and animals, no witches flying through the air, and, most importantly, no sexual abuse of young children.

Nevertheless, these "scandals" had a profound impact on the American psyche. Many people were convinced that satanic ritual abuse was at work among our most vulnerable populations. But we also learned, over time, that false memories can be implanted in people, especially those with young and impressionable minds. The interviewing techniques used with children in the McMartin case were found to be highly suggestive, even coercive, encouraging the children to pretend or speculate about what might have happened. This led to fraudulent accusations resulting from false memory syndrome. Initially, based on such testimony, it was claimed that 360 children had been abused. In the end, the truth was that none had been mistreated. A 1996 investigation of more than 12,000 allegations of satanic, ritual, and religious abuse resulted in NO cases that were considered factual or corroborated.

I was the victim of this hysteria and the resulting fraudulent practice, starting with Dr. Doom when I was a teenager, and continuing with the horrors I experienced at Fantasy Island with Mr. Roarke. They were convinced that my eating disorder was the result of childhood sexual abuse. They were determined to discover that abuse by probing my memories and subconscious. In the case of Fantasy Island, Mr. Roarke was absolutely certain that I was engaged in ritualized Satanism, among other bizarre practices. The key to curing me was to identify my repressed memories (and multiple personalities) and bring them into the light of day.

This book isn't just about me. It's about the 30 million Americans and 70 million individuals worldwide affected by eating disorders. Nearly half of all Americans personally know someone with an eating disorder. This is an epidemic of monumental proportions. A crisis.

This chapter is a call for action. I'm going to look at the incompetent, almost criminal ways in which my eating disorder was treated, the evidence-based treatments that worked, and what we need to change about our healthcare system—the fights that all of us have to fight.

In fact, we don't have a healthcare system to fix—it has to be established. Now!

The Hoax of Recovered Memory Therapy

Although Roarke didn't call it hypnosis, that was the technique he used on me. Defined broadly, hypnosis is any intentionally or unintentionally induced trance state, which can include age regression, relaxation, and guided imagery exercises. But any memories "recovered" during hypnosis are of limited reliability, at best.

Science writer Mark Pendergrast, the foremost expert on the subject, explores the brain and its billions of synaptic connections, explaining how memories are formed, stored throughout the brain, subject to contamination, and reconstructed. In understandable terms, Pendergrast explains the difference between explicit and implicit memory, the phenomenon of infantile amnesia, and much more.

In this chapter I quote liberally from Pendergrast's 600-page textbook *The Repressed Memory Epidemic: How it Happened and What We Need to Learn from It*. He explores how, over the past century, the most dangerous and damaging of all forms of psychotherapy have been "repressed memory therapy" (RMT) and "multiple personality disorder" (MPD) therapy. Thousands of patients who sought help for simple depression and anxiety were instead hypnotized, threatened, manipulated, and/or drugged into believing horrific, false memories of childhood abuse.

It appears that the apparent vividness of hypnotic recall can crystallize imagined events and give them the appearance of memory. Summarizing the relevant studies on the topic, the Council on Scientific Affairs of the American Medical Association published a warning that hypnotically repressed memories could not be relied on. "Contrary to what is generally believed by the public, recollections obtained during hypnosis not only fail to be more accurate but actually appear to be generally less reliable than recall." The report, published in the Journal of the American Medical Association in 1985, went on to conclude that "in no study to date has there been an increase in accuracy associated with an appropriate increase in confidence in the veracity of recollections. Consequently, hypnosis may increase the appearance of certitude without a concurrent increase of veracity." Similar observations have led other researchers into hypnosis to define the state as one of "believed-in imaginings."

When Roarke said hypnosis was necessary, I knew little to nothing about it other than what was portrayed by the entertainment industry. I had no idea I had jumped on a yellow brick road to madness. I was so desperate to uncover the mystery of my eating disorder that I believed him without question. At the time, several ED treatment centers promoted the effectiveness of hypnosis, all without data backing up this claim.

Pendergrast again:

The other possible explanation for the lack of observable symptoms at the beginning of treatment is that the symptoms don't exist at the beginning of therapy. As Dr. Paul McHugh, director of the Department of Psychiatry and Behavioral Science at Johns Hopkins Medical Institution, states concisely, this possibility leads to the conclusion that "MPD (DID) is an iatrogenic behavior syndrome, promoted by suggestion and maintained by clinical attention, social consequences, and group loyalties."

Roarke had successfully treated thousands of cult survivors through recovered memory therapy, he told me with pride. I was like a blister "that needed to be popped to cure." (Yeah, he said that.) In reality, he trapped me in a vast lie. As Pendergrast writes:

Dr. Paul McHugh of Johns Hopkins has proposed that there is something of a civil war within the mental-health field between romantics who rely on inspiration and myth, and empiricists who argue that practice in the mental-health field should be based on scientific observation and methodical study of patients. "The empiricists are winning because their approach has expanded, in a clear and gratifying way, our knowledge of mental disorders," he writes, adding that the romantics are losing because "as romantics will, they have become infatuated by their own thoughts. They claim to know things they never try to prove. They are charmed by novelty and ignore, even disdain, drab facts. More recently, in their thinking they have taken a nightmarish turn towards chaos that has caused patients and their families much suffering."

Mr. Roarke to the T. No research. No proof. No track record. Just a long-haired crank in a flowing robe infatuated with his insane theories.

Mr. Roarke was in a powerful position. I thought of him as godlike. I was undernourished, starved, and terribly overmedicated, which made me susceptible to an unwavering belief in him. He was my savior, I was convinced without question. In the privacy of his office, with no regulation in sight, he chose to play god with my psyche.

Pendergrast:

One would think that such whopping bills would have alerted parsimonious insurance companies, who would then send their investigators, but that was not the case. Some insurance companies actually owned stock in private psychiatric hospitals, a clear conflict of interest. In addition, according to one angry psychiatrist, insurance companies like large bills. "Big bills mean big premiums and bonuses," a doctor working for a major insurer observed. Finally, insurance officials were often afraid to crack down on mental health fraud. "Insurance companies are petrified [of mental illness]," one expert testified before a congressional committee in 1992. "They don't want to touch it. They don't understand it. All you have to do is threaten to sue them or push them and they back down." Besides, why should they worry about it when they could pass on the bill to corporations and taxpayers?

A travesty beyond measure. Would a functioning and equitable mental health system have prevented such negligence and lack of appropriate care? YES, period. But we don't have a mental health system—period. Can you hear me?

Roarke even wrote a letter to Hawkeye after I left Fantasy Island following my psychotic break. This letter stated my drawings were suspect and encouraged my return. Roarke added that my insurance would cover my treatment, i.e., continue to line his pockets.

As Pendergrast notes:

Money also flowed freely into the coffers of recovered memory therapists directly from the government spigot. In a biographical sketch, MPD specialist Colin Ross bragged that he had received "several hundred thousand dollars in research funding." Despite the clear evidence that facilitated communication does not work. Consistent with the long history of fads, frauds, and quackery, and the nearly total absence of competent patient protections or licensing systems in the mental health field, many thousands of patients fell prey to these evil therapies as entire hospital units in multiple states were devoted to such harmful but lucrative practices.

What Pendergrast describes fit exactly what I had suffered at Fantasy Island:

The personal, familial, and social damage from RMT and MPD therapies constituted the worst epidemic of quackery in the history of the mental health system. The millions of persons harmed directly or indirectly by RMT and MPD therapies created a vast tsunami of suffering far beyond that of the estimated 50,000 victims of the cruel brain surgery known as lobotomy.

If you were an automobile manufacturer and discovered that one model had a fatally flawed part, would you simply stop manufacturing the car, or would you recall the faulty vehicles? If you were a doctor and prescribed medicine that you subsequently discovered was poison, would you just stop dispensing it, or would you warn patients who might still be taking it?

A Fantasy Island employee who quit in 2013 estimated that half of the patients wound up with recovered memories of abuse: "Most got profoundly more disturbed by being there."

Pendregrast again:

In the hundreds of files I reviewed, patients always got worse—and often much worse—during this process. Therapists often told patients descending into suicidal despair that they "had to get worse and recover more memories of abuse before they could get better." Gullible, desperate patients thus continued the debilitating search for ever-more "memories" as the therapist continually reminded and threatened the desperate patients that recovering more memories was the only way they could ever get well.

Please be assured that I'm not denying the existence of devastating trauma and sexual abuse, which can have lifelong negative effects on a person's life. I *am* denying those memories manufactured by therapists. The memories "recovered" in therapy were remarkably consistent throughout the world because RMT-MPD therapists read the same training materials, attended the same training conferences, and used the same dangerous training materials on patients.

Pendergrast thoroughly investigated this fraud:

In my years of investigation, I never found any of the recovered memory reports to be accurate. Patients who claimed to have given birth for "cult sacrifices" had medical records proving they had never given birth. Many victims of RMT and MPD therapies lost jobs, marriages, and their sanity.

The second question asked by almost all journalists was: "Why did the therapists use such damaging methods and procedures?" The answer is that most RMT-MPD therapists actually thought they were helping patients, though they were invariably poorly trained in the basic science of memory and hypnosis and were often very troubled themselves. It should also be said the RMT-MPD business was very lucrative indeed. A 30-year-old mother with mild depression would typically require a dozen sessions of cognitive-behavioral therapy to be well. Turning such a patient into a suicidal, depressed survivor of cult abuse, with a hundred alter personalities, would require years of hospitalization and treatments costing hundreds of thousands of dollars.

[T]he idea—that people can "repress" or "dissociate" years of traumatic childhood memories and then recall them as adults—refused to die, in part because it provides an appealing plot device for novels, movies, and sensational media coverage, and because many psychologists have imbibed the theory somewhat like mother's milk.

Given the powerful ideological and political

movements pushing the epidemic, and the enormous financial rewards involved in turning a depressed housewife into an MPD patient needing years of expensive hospitalizations, scientific information was insufficient to halt the burgeoning international epidemic of false memories. But repressed memory theory was pure pseudoscience, a matter of faith rather than anything that can be proved or disproved.

Here is an unequivocal passage from the 1989 fifth edition of the *Comprehensive Textbook of Psychiatry*:

An overwhelming body of research indicates that hypnosis does not increase accurate memory but does increase the person's willingness to report previously uncertain memories with strong conviction. Furthermore, the hypnotized individual has a pronounced tendency to confabulate in those areas where there is little or no recollection; to distort memory to become more congruent with beliefs ... and fantasies; and to incorporate cues from leading questions as factual memories. Finally, there is a high likelihood that the beliefs of the hypnotist will somehow be communicated to the patient in hypnosis and incorporated into what the patient believes to be memories, often with strong conviction.

Exactly what happened on Fantasy Island, although I found out only after reprehensible damage was done. As Pendergrast writes:

Many therapists considered eating disorders a nearly fool-proof symptom of childhood incest. A woman's therapist told her that 80% of all eating-disorder patients had been sexually abused. Yet there is no scientific evidence that eating disorders stem from childhood molestation, as Harvard psychiatrists Harrison Pope and James Hudson, specialists in the field, repeatedly stressed. Despite such findings, thousands of vulnerable women desperate for help with their eating disorders continued to search for repressed memories.

My heart aches for these victims. In conjunction with Roarke's suggestive therapy, I was severely overmedicated during my time on Fantasy Island. Drugs can significantly increase the likelihood of illusory sex abuse memories. Even without overt suggestion, physicians and therapists have long recognized that strong sedative compounds can lead to false accusations. It was clearly a major ingredient in the recipe of my demise.

The other major fraud perpetrated on me at Fantasy Island was my diagnosis of MPD or DID—that I harbored several distinct personalities within my body and brain.

Pendergrast again:

The most extreme claims of repressed memories involved supposed ritual abuse, and they almost invariably led to a diagnosis of multiple personality disorder, otherwise known as MPD, now renamed dissociative identity disorder (DID). First "diagnosed" around the turn of the [20th] century, multiple personalities were considered rare until the publication of *The Three Faces of Eve* by Thigpen and Cleckley in 1957. Their book told the story of "Eve," in reality Christine Costner Sizemore, who ultimately graduated from 3 to 22 different internal personalities. But it was *Sybil*, published in 1973 and made into a popular movie in 1977, that really spawned the modern crop of multiples and provided the cornerstone for an assumed background of sexual abuse.

Surprisingly, many MPD clients appeared to be "high-functioning," seemingly normal individuals who were themselves completely unaware that they harbored multiple alters. Only under hypnosis or through suggestive interviewing did they reveal themselves to the savvy therapist, who could then question each personality, calling them forward in turn. The therapists were usually alerted to the possibility of MPD when their patients reported an inability to remember whole chunks of their childhood. These cases often progressed in stages. First, the patient revealed simple repressed memories of abuse, often by a father or grandfather. Then, hints of far worse horrors surfaced. Eventually, these patients remembered ritual group abuse, often involving worship of Satan. In a group setting, they were purportedly subjected to hideous sexual and physical abuse. As part of the ritual, babies were hacked to death and eaten, blood and urine drunk, feces consumed, and every other conceivable horror experienced.

As we now know—as I now know—none of this behavior was true, but rather the fantasy of charlatans, self-appointed saviors, and crooks.

In its code of conduct, published in 1992, the American Psychological Association called for informed consent that would provide "significant information concerning the procedure" to clients who then "freely and without undue influence express consent." But as the repressed memory epidemic has demonstrated, that code has never been enforced. In 1996, the American Psychiatric Association failed to demand informed consent of psychiatric patients, observing, "There has always been uncertainty as the extent to which the doctrine of informed consent is applicable to psychotherapy." Never throughout all my years of treatment was I adequately informed about the procedures I was forced to endure.

Believe it or not, the repressed memory epidemic continues today, although at a reduced pace, conducted mostly by poorly trained—but often fully licensed— Psy.D. (not Ph.D.) psychologists, social worker therapists, massage therapists, and fringe religion counselors. A quick search of the Internet will find chat rooms, blogs, articles in the popular press, and allegedly professional societies still espousing beliefs in RMT-MPD. Credulous and incompetent younger practitioners have picked up where others have left off.

Whether through legislation or through actions by the professional associations, the standards should be strengthened for those who call themselves psychotherapists or hypnotists. On the federal or state level, a single law should be enacted to cover all psychotherapists. Currently, each state hosts a hodgepodge of regulatory peer review boards for psychiatrists, psychologists, social workers, marriage and family counselors, and the like. Most do a poor job of monitoring or punishing their peers. Usually, the fringe therapists using past life regression or channeling are completely unregulated.

Standards should require a specified level of education from accredited institutions, periodic continuing education in approved subjects, and ongoing observation and review. Such education should specifically include research on human suggestibility and the dangers of repressed memory therapy. Review boards should include members of the public, elected officials, and psychologists. To avoid a rubber-stamp peer review, the number of psychologists should not constitute a majority on any board.

As Professor Walter Mischel, former President of the Association for Psychological Science, recently noted: "The disconnect between much of clinical practice and the advances in psychological science is an unconscionable embarrassment to the profession." My experience offers proof that he was correct.

I'll let Mark Pendergrast have the final word:

It is important that we learn from the past and not "repress" the memories of what amounted to a modern witch hunt in the late twentieth century.

Chapter Eleven

We Need a
Mental Health System

When I say we need a mental health system, I mean exactly that. In my view, we don't have one right now. We need to create a functional, equitable, and patient-centered system from the ground up, a unified and compassionate system that replaces the various and opposing silos that currently exist.

In this chapter, I will review my opinions on the major challenges facing our existing healthcare system and what we must do to create a world-class system, not only to treat eating disorders humanely, but all mental illnesses.

In 1948, the World Health Organization defined health as "a state of complete physical, mental and social well-being and not simply the absence of disease." More than 75 years later, our medical system continues to treat the mind and body separately, without regard for the overall needs of the patient. The absence of integrated mental healthcare and medical healthcare poses a serious health risk to millions of patients and needs to be remedied.

Mental Illness and the Treatment Gap

Eating disorders are just as prevalent as or more prevalent than breast cancer, HIV, Alzheimer's, and schizophrenia. Anorexia is the third most common chronic illness among young people, after asthma and type one diabetes (National Eating Disorders Association, NEDA), with 42% of first to third grade girls wanting to be thinner and 81% of 10-year-olds afraid of being fat. Heartbreaking. Americans spend over $40 billion on dieting and diet related products each year. And middle-aged women are the fastest growing segment of the population being diagnosed with eating disorders.

Every 62 minutes in the U.S., at least one person dies as a direct result from an eating disorder. Anorexia has the highest mortality rate of all mental illnesses. Suicide, depression, and severe anxiety are common among people with EDs.

One in five adults in America (20%) experience a mental illness. Ninety percent of those who die by suicide have an underlying mental illness. Some 16 million American adults live with major depression, and 42 million American adults live with anxiety disorders.

Suicide is the 10th leading cause of death in the U.S. Thirty percent of all suicides were committed by pre-teen to young adults, with suicide being the 2nd leading cause of death in the 10-to 34-year-old group. In spite of federal and local attempts to prevent teen suicide it is increasing every year, particularly in rural areas. In 2016, 13,525 of our youth died as the result of suicide. Tragic. Heartbreaking. Clearly early intervention is necessary. This cannot be ignored. In the U.S., someone dies from suicide every 14 minutes.

Serious mental illness costs America $193.2 billion in lost earnings every year. This is not the total cost. Treatment costs for mental illnesses are $201 billion annually. The CDC estimates that mood disorders will account for 50% of hospital admittances in 2020. The cost of attempted suicides and suicides is $96.3 billion, totaling $490.5 billion. This is four times the federal education budget.

When compared with other illnesses, mental illness costs the most to treat. It costs $58 billion more than heart conditions and $148 billion more than diabetes.

But where is our mental health system in responding to this crisis? Millions of people are falling through the cracks. Nearly 60% of adults and 50% of youth with a mental illness didn't receive mental health services in the previous year. It bears repeating— only 41% of adults in the U.S. with a mental health condition received treatment in the past year. Barriers to treatment include cost, access, the desperate need for parity, and the pervasive stigma that continues to run wild.

For years, medical professionals blamed me for my disorder. I was treated with contempt. Why was I "flagrantly anorexic"? Why was I using my ED as an attention-seeking device? Why wasn't I smart enough or tough enough or resourceful enough to master my demons? Why was I choosing to starve myself? I was labeled a lost cause by so-called professionals who offered no answers, understanding, or help.

When we plant flowers and they don't grow well, we never blame the flowers. We blame the conditions— the soil, the climate, the lack of nourishment and precipitation—that caused the flowers not to bloom. To extend this metaphor, why do we blame the person who has a mental illness? Why don't we look at the causes and conditions of the disease? Too often, in our society, we ignore the causes, blame the victim, and provide inadequate treatment. Health care providers aren't well-trained in referring people to mental health professionals.

People with mental illness are dehumanized; their legitimate concerns are trivialized. This prejudice creates great barriers to effective distribution of mental health services. Individuals and families are often afraid, embarrassed, and too ashamed to seek help. The average delay between the onset of symptoms of mental illness and intervention is eight to 10 years!

Only a small percentage of people affected by eating disorders, estimated at one-third, receive the treatment they need to recover (Eating Disorders Coalition, EDC). Let's hear that stat again—70% of people with EDs receive no treatment at all. Only one in five of adolescents with EDs receives treatment (just 20%). How can we not be outraged? All illnesses deserve timely treatment, but eating disorder treatment resources are far less available than for other serious illnesses. In addition, research funding is drastically disproportionate.

Eating disorders *can* be successfully and fully treated through evidence-based psychosocial interventions. It is estimated that most individuals need from three to six months of inpatient care, not the lengthy institutionalization that almost destroyed my life. But adequate resources are scarce. ED treatment centers spend a fortune on PR and marketing to outdo their competitors. They manufacture "success rates" to maintain a cycle of repeat business. It was this kind of promotion that fooled me into thinking Fantasy Island was a reputable program. If the treatment centers are so effective, why then is there so much repeat business? My heart breaks again for the millions who receive either shoddy treatment or no treatment at all.

According to current scientific evidence, mental illness is essentially biological in nature and is sometimes triggered by environmental factors such as trauma. This defies the myth that such illnesses result from a failure of character and will. Mental illness affects a person's behavior but the illness is not "behavioral," which implies that it's a matter of choice.

We must do more to educate the public that mental illness is not due to lack of will. It's a brain disease that needs treatment and people shouldn't be ashamed to seek that treatment.

It was not until I was in my forties that I finally

realized, with Hawkeye's wise help, that people have a genetic predisposition toward EDs. In fact, it's estimated that developing an eating disorder is 50% to 80% determined by genetics.

This provided me with enormous relief, after over 30 years of battling and blaming myself. It wasn't my fault, after all. But genetics does not spell destiny. We have the power to conquer our demons, if we receive the proper support and care.

We need a mental health system that destigmatizes mental illness and that provides quality care to everyone who needs it.

Environmental Factors

We live in a media saturated world. Diet commercials are constantly telling us that once we lose weight, we'll be happy. Models and even mannequins provide images of emaciated women. While current research indicates that environmental factors alone cannot cause an eating disorder, millions of people are spending billions and starving themselves to achieve the ideal figure that the fashion industry and society dangle before their eyes.

Can we modify these environmental factors? Can we lessen the dangerous media influence that's killing people? We must. We certainly must try. We must resist the temptation to accept, uncritically, distorted and unhealthy images of who we should be.

Mercifully some conscientious advertisers have begun using healthy people with varying body types in their ads. Thank you! We need much more of this.

Evidence-Based Treatment

The National Alliance on Mental Illness (NAMI) believes that individuals with mental illnesses must have access to treatments that have been recognized as effective by the Food and Drug Administration (FDA) and the National Institute of Mental Health (NIMH).

NAMI is also adamant that individuals with mental illness have access to clinically appropriate medications, evidence-based services, and treatments, including psychotherapy, that are provided in a person-centered approach.

With evidence-based treatment, a provider can assess the strength of the evidence to tell if the treatment works. The provider can also assess the risks and benefits of ordering diagnostic tests and treatments for each patient. Such an approach, coupled with the provider's clinical experience, enables them to better predict if a treatment will do more harm than good. Not exactly the approach followed at Fantasy Island, where there was zero transparency and accountability.

I never experienced adequate care—clinically sound and scientifically-based care—until I started seeing Hawkeye. His treatment plan involved proper levels of medication, cognitive behavioral therapy, and exposure therapy to cure my agoraphobia. He believed I had to learn coping skills on an outpatient basis, not in an institution. Controlled research has clearly demonstrated that cognitive and behavioral therapies are more effective than other approaches in treating EDs.

Cognitive therapy concentrates on current problems rather than rehashing and reinterpreting the past. Cognitive therapists stress how people's belief systems—the ways they think about themselves and others—interfere with their lives. By reframing and modifying self-defeating attitudes, people can better cope with their lives

Hawkeye helped change the obsessive and negative ways of thinking that had become ingrained in me. He addressed, with great care and patience, the particular roadblocks that stood in my way. Through evidence-based treatments like nutrition education and physiological education, he addressed my fears about changing dangerous behaviors.

Yet only 35% of treatments provided by residential treatment centers are evidence-based, according to the IBIS World US Market Research Report on Eating Disorder Clinics (November 2016). How is this acceptable? Where is the accountability? Where is real, comprehensive oversight? We're not talking about used car dealers, but a business that's responsible for treating a deadly disease.

We need a mental health system that stresses evidence-based treatments and that provides the public with the resources to choose the best treatments for their conditions.

A Big Business with No Accountability

The ED treatment industry is huge and very profitable. A U.S. Market Research Report provides revealing statistics. Annual revenue of one billion. Annual growth of 6.6%. Employment at 8,515. More than 411 treatment centers.

But accountability? Very little. My state has more than most, but even then, it's not adequate. There's a complex complaint system that's hard to navigate by someone who's in emotional distress. A complaint system doesn't lead to accountability and oversight.

There needs to be a mandated federal standard of care and oversight when it comes to treatment centers. Right now, most ED treatment centers self-regulate themselves. My insurance company kept paying for numerous prescriptions that kept me in a medicated fog without any discernable improvement. Who was approving this nonsense? Was anyone watching? Checking my pulse?

In my case, insurance companies were paying for treatments I shouldn't have had and weren't paying for what I needed. You can blame Fantasy Island for what I and many others suffered, but they couldn't have subjected us to their inhumane treatment if our insurance companies hadn't paid for it recklessly in the wake of the effort and passing of the parity law.

Appalling. Even more appalling is that no regulatory body can stop the use of recovered memory therapy, even though it's a bogus practice that has caused enormous harm. We no longer allow physicians to bleed patients with leeches as a cure for pneumonia. Why/how do we allow quackery to persist in treating anorexia?

Ultimately, a measurement-based care culture

should lead to greater accountability for mental health services, regardless of where the consumer enters the system. In addition, we need to improve strategies to foster accountability in performance improvement. The public reporting of performance is vital for holding health care organizations accountable for improving care.

Mental health programs and providers have not fully embraced quality measurement due to infrastructure and policy impediments intrinsic to mental health, "cookbook medicine," and the silos across different provider types and credentialing requirements.

We need ONE standard for accreditation.

And we need ironclad accountability and oversight! It's interesting that the American Medical Association has been able to take a far stronger stand on this issue than the professions most directly implicated in the problem. Since the AMA principally represents physicians who practice specialties other than psychiatry, fewer of its members have a vested interest in ignoring the recovered memory epidemic. In fact, way back in June 1994, the AMA passed a resolution warning of the dangers of false memories being "recovered" by memory therapy.

We need a health care system that is carefully monitored and held to the highest standards of accountability.

Mental Health Parity and Insurance Issues

Over ten years ago, in October 2008, Congress passed the Mental Health Parity and Addiction Equity Act, requiring private insurance plans to provide coverage for mental health and substance abuse treatment on an equivalent basis with other medical or surgical benefits IF the plan covers mental health or substance use disorder treatment. IF? Unbelievable. It's immoral for insurance companies to discriminate against people with mental illness, yet only a handful of states at this time have implemented mental health parity laws. How can this be justified? Equal access to mental health and addiction treatment services is our right!

ParityTrack, a collaborative forum led by former Surgeon General Dr. David Satcher, author of the *Surgeon General's Report on Mental Health*, and the Hon. Patrick J. Kennedy, monitors the implementation of parity and educates consumers about it. ParityTrack has noted:

As rates of suicides and overdoses continue

to climb nationwide, mental health parity is more important than ever. Unfortunately, studies have shown that many insurers are still not in compliance with the Federal Parity Law. A 2017 report by Milliman confirmed that reimbursement rates for mental health and substance use disorder treatment providers, through private insurance plans, were far lower than reimbursement rates for other medical providers, relative to Medicare rates. When insurance plans do not reimburse providers adequately, many choose not to participate in the plans' networks. So, when someone makes a decision to seek help – yet they are unable to find a provider in network – they often have to go out-of-network, resulting in higher costs. Many people give up simply because they can't afford treatment. For this and other reasons, parity has become a human rights issue.

My state is still not adequately enforcing mental health parity regulations and was recently given a failing grade from the Kennedy Forum. Our chapter of the National Alliance for Mental Illness (NAMI) supports passing substantial legislation to ensure that private insurance plans can no longer discriminate against people with mental illnesses.

The law must be enforced. We need monitoring with strict oversight to ensure accountability. We need standardized measures that allow results of compliance to be monitored and tracked uniformly. Health plans cannot be allowed to charge more for mental health care than other forms of health care, which they do. Health plans cannot be allowed to set arbitrary treatment limits for mental health care, which they do.

In recent years it has become much harder to go to a therapist, psychologist, or treatment center because the insurance industry has really tamped down on how much they pay for therapy and psychiatric treatment. According to the American Psychiatric Association (2017), Milliman researchers discovered that physical healthcare providers were paid, on average, about 20% higher rates than behavioral health providers for the very same office visits billed under identical or similar codes. In many states, the disparities in payment rates were 2-3 times greater, a factor likely influencing network access and the overall availability of in-network practitioners. With mental illness not covered to the same extent as physical diseases, many people are left untreated. Adding to the problem is that mental health treatment is more expensive for the public because of co-pays, deductibles, and out-of-pocket costs for medication.

With greater access to outpatient mental health care, more people with a mental illness will stay out of hospitals, leading to better outcomes and lower long-term costs for the health care system.

We need a healthcare system that provides equal and quality treatment for physical and mental illness.

The Need for Insurance Industry Reform

Parity Track notes seven common parity violations that need to be addressed through insurance reform:

Insurer requires patient to pay a separate deductible or higher co-pays for mental health services.

Insurer sets limits on how many days a patient can stay in a treatment facility or how many times they can see a mental health provider.

Insurer charges more for prescription medication for mental health treatment.

Insurer makes patient get permission before starting and/or continuing treatment.

Insurer forces patient to try a less expensive treatment before pursuing treatment recommended by a doctor.

Insurer refuses to pay for residential mental health treatment recommended by a doctor.

Insurer refuses to pay for mental health treatment outside of patient's state or region.

Why? Lack of federal regulation and enforcement. Period. We need a universal framework for enforcement, quality monitoring, and accountability. In essence, elected officials should do their jobs for ALL of America.

If your insurance plan does not offer coverage for mental health and substance abuse services, or if this coverage is not equal to your other benefits, don't accept this. You have to be your own advocate and there are steps you can take. Call your insurance benefits department. Call your state insurance commissioner. Finally, file a complaint with the federal government. Go to http://www/hhs.gov/parity for more information on this process and helpful phone numbers.

It's worth repeating that more than ten years have passed since the Mental Health and Addiction Equity Act was signed into law by President George W. Bush.

Former Congressman Patrick J. Kennedy, a member of the President's Commission on Combating Drug Addiction and the Opioid Crisis, author of the Mental Health Parity and Addiction Equity Act, and founder of The Kennedy Forum, has said: "If nearly 300 people dying each day from overdoses and suicides isn't sufficient to motivate insurers to take immediate action to improve access to the full range of in-network benefits, we have a real problem – and it's time to start holding them publicly accountable."

Nationally, researchers at Milliman, among the world's largest consulting firms, have found that in 2015, on average:

–**31.6%** of outpatient facility behavioral health care was accessed out-of-network, while only **5.5%** of outpatient facility medical/surgical care was accessed out-of-network. In 2013, the out-of-network outpatient facility use for behavioral health was **15.6%**, showing a **doubling** of access restrictions during three years of parity regulatory oversight.

–**18.7%** of behavioral health office visits were accessed out-of-network, while only **3.7%** of primary medical/surgical office visits were accessed out-of-network.

–**16.7%** of inpatient facility behavioral health care was accessed out-of-network, while only **4.0%** of inpatient facility medical/surgical care was accessed out-of-network.

"The numbers tell a story, and it's a painful one for those seeking treatment for mental illness or addiction," said Mary Giliberti, former CEO of the National Alliance on Mental Illness. "Behind those numbers are millions of Americans who can't get the care they desperately need. We are confident that this Milliman analysis has uncovered a key barrier to network access—unfairly low reimbursement payments to mental health and addiction providers."

Other highlights from the Milliman report include:

–As of 2015, out-of-network use of behavioral health inpatient care (as compared to medical care) was approximately **800% higher** in California, New York, and Rhode Island, and over **1000% higher** in Connecticut, Florida, New Jersey, Pennsylvania, and New Hampshire. These states collectively comprise 30% of the U.S. population.

–In 2015, there were 24 states with reimbursement disparities ranging from 30% to 69%, including Washington, Kentucky, and Virginia.

A coalition of major mental health advocacy groups urges the following immediate action steps:

–Federal Regulators should issue more specific guidance on medical management practices with examples of compliant analyses and, based on this report's findings, should immediately initiate audits of major insurers.

–Employers should retain independent companies to conduct parity compliance audits of the insurance plans provided to their employees in order to measure reimbursements, out-of-network use, denial rates, and other key variables restricting access to benefits.

–State-level agencies should conduct routine annual parity compliance market audits of all insurers in their state, for both commercial and Medicaid-managed care companies.

How We Can Help

Are you left wondering how you can help? We can all listen, learn, and use the power of our collective voices. Let's break down the barriers to care with one powerful voice. We can be loud enough to be heard. We can all fight to remove the dangerous and pervasive stigma around mental illness that prevents people from seeking lifesaving help. We can demand adequate funding for mental health research. We can fight for real healthcare reform. We can ensure that people are treated with evidence-based care and not quackery.

The first step in making change is to educate yourself about the mental health crisis. In order to spread the word and raise awareness, you have to understand what mental illness is and what it looks like. What are the warning signs and symptoms? How can mental illness be successfully treated? What are the public policy issues around mental illness, the legal and civil rights issues, as well as funding issues? How can research lead to more effective treatments? A great source of information on these topics is the National Alliance on Mental Illness (NAMI) (nami.org).

When you are informed, you can then inform and educate others, and become actively involved in trying to make change.

The best way to do that is to start local, on the grassroots level. Perhaps you have a story to tell about yourself or someone you know who has been affected by this issue. Share your story—you are not alone. We all have authentic voices that must be heard.

Talk with your community leaders to raise awareness. Reach out to the faith community and local businesses. Speak at the local library, or at a community organization, or to your local community government. Even host an event.

You can tell your story to legislators and other elected officials, which brings us to advocacy, a major way we can make a difference. Call, email, or write a letter to your local, state, and federal legislators. You can also meet with them, to put a face on the issue, a real person with a real story.

When meeting with elected officials:
- Be on time.
- Introduce yourself and tell your story.
- Speak from personal experience about why you are there.
- Ask them for their position on a particular issue or bill, and how they will vote if a bill is pending.
- Explain why you agree or disagree with their position.
- Thank them for their time.
- Promptly write a thank you note.

Letters are also effective and easier than meeting in person. Again, sharing a personal story has the largest impact. When writing letters to elected officials:

- Keep them to one page.
- Clearly identify the issue that concerns you.
- Discuss only one issue per letter.
- Get right to the point. Discuss how the issue/
- legislation affects you. Share a personal story about the challenges you've faced.
- Thank them for their time.
- Include your contact information.
- In writing a letter, you can follow this general outline:

  Paragraph 1: State why you are writing.
  Paragraph 2: State your interest on the issue.
  Paragraph 3: State your position on the issue.
  Paragraph 4: Ask for action.
  Paragraph 5: Thank them for their time.

You can also call, following the above outline. Keep your call to five minutes.

In writing a letter to a newspaper, follow this format:
- Keep it under 250 words.
- Respond to a single current issue.
- Write as though you're talking directly to the editor; speak personally and from the heart.
- Include contact information.

Use your voice. With united perseverance, we have the power to accomplish constructive and sustainable change.

Remember the words of Margaret Mead: "Never doubt that a small group of thoughtful, committed citizens can change the world; indeed, it's the only thing that ever has."

Chapter Twelve

I'm On My Way, Hell Yeah

"I freed my soul—just let it fly."
–Neil Diamond

Time to get off my soap box. I'm afraid of heights anyway. I've learned I'm not a lost cause. Nobody is. With Hawkeye's help, I finally realized that I never was. I've been sustained by the love of my family, who never gave up on me despite my darkest of days, when I pushed everyone away and hid under the covers.

Which I still do at times. My struggle isn't over by any means. My wounds and scars continue to haunt me. Still fighting the fog. The mirror remains my enemy. Trying to love my body, the only one I'll ever have. I have to remember it's precious and resilient. It's working for me all the time. I have been at war with my body for far too long. After years of torment, I have had enough! I'm only human. Flesh and bones. Mortal like everyone else. My body deserves respect and kindness for all it does. Hawkeye reminds me of this.

Despite the fog that still looms and scares me, despite my great anxiety and self-doubt, I have jumped into public speaking. Telling my story to fight against the stigma of mental illness, the lack of understanding, the ignorance and discrimination, and to fight for proper mental health treatment for all. I'm no longer ashamed, as I was most of my life.

I have to thank Hawkeye for giving me the nudge that made me come alive. One of my assignments in therapy was to face one of my biggest fears by getting out of my house periodically. But when I volunteered at a local ED foundation, I was put to work doing data entry. Quite discouraging. Ridiculous indeed. I had so much more to offer.

So I turned to NAMI (National Alliance on Mental Illness). I thought telling my story might help people, if just a few. They have speaking programs to educate various audiences about mental illness. I facilitate peer support groups at a local hospital. I have received my Certification as a Peer Support Specialist. I want to do all I can to make sure nobody suffers from the treatment I received.

It takes me hours to gather the strength to speak

and facilitate my groups. The night before, the anxiety begins. Anxiety about leaving the house. About telling my story. About standing before an audience. But I fight that anxiety with all my might. I always arrive a half hour early to meet the coordinator and gather any helpful information. My breathing is shallow, my pulse increases, and my palms become sweaty, yet I know what I have to do. What I desperately want to do. Once I begin, my strength surfaces. Most of the time.

I enter the room and access my surroundings, hoping my anti-anxiety meds remain helpful. Introductions begin, and I try to use my dry wit to alleviate my tension.

When telling my personal story, my format is "What Happened – What Helped – What's Next." All eyes are on me. I walk as I talk to allay my nervousness and engage the audience to personalize my message. My voice becomes steadier, less emotional. Yet animated with passion. Any questions? I'm terrified as hands go up. Questions about meds. About suicide attempts and ideation. What caused my anorexia. About the changes needed in mental health care.

It's hard to remember all the questions I'm asked as I'm extremely nervous I won't have the answers and want to flee. But after the audience breaks up at the end, I'm always confronted by people giving thanks and expressing awe that I could share my story. Asking questions that hadn't been asked before. Telling me they have a loved one suffering from mental illness. Sometimes giving me hugs. I collect the questionnaires and dash out to my car. Sometimes I cry (not exactly sure why). I reflect on those I touched. It takes me time to calm down after, but it always feels worth it. Fills my heart with gratitude that I affected some lives. Found my voice.

I will never forget a meeting I spoke at in a relatively small town. A woman asked the speaker before me about where she could find resources for her younger son, who was suffering from mental illness due to the suicide of his older brother two years before. Her voice quivered with emotion as she asked her question. The speaker responded by referring her to an organization's website. I saw the woman's head drop in defeat.

I approached this woman right after the meeting finished, asking if I could help with any questions that hadn't been answered. Her eyes were haunted as they met mine. She began to cry, and we stepped outside of the auditorium. When she told me about her son's death, my tears flowed as well. She now feared for her younger son's life if he couldn't find psychiatric treatment. I gave her more specific information to help with her problem, and as we talked, we cried. I told her I wished there was much more I could do. She thanked me profusely and simply asked for a hug.

I speak before groups of police officers who are receiving Critical Incidence Training (CIT). "I'm Lisa," I'll begin. "I'm a rookie, so please bear with me. I'm a recovered PR and politico professional." Which elicits a laugh. Again, my heart is pounding and my hands are sweaty and shaking. I try to explain anorexia, depression, and anxiety. Very honest about my continuing struggles as recovery is not linear.

"Do you think an eating disorder is really a mental illness?" an officer asked. Flustered, I responded, "Yes indeed, and it has the highest mortality rate of any mental illness."

"Are suicide attempts a call for help or a real intention?"

I responded with a bit of defiance: "Some may be a desperate call for help or playing Russian roulette. But any attempt means that someone finds it more painful to live than to die."

Silence filled the room. Then the last comment: "You don't have the face of mental illness. Thank you for sharing your story." I was taken aback. A thank you? A realization that there is no "face" to mental illness? I had gotten my message through and that made it worthwhile.

The more I spoke to groups, the easier it became. I have become much more comfortable. I was able to make eye contact more easily and speak alone, without a co-facilitator. The questions have become easier to answer. Yet I still spend significant time gathering the strength to do this.

I also advocate for people with eating disorders and other mental health issues through legislative efforts. I serve on the legislative committee as part of our chapter of NAMI, which focuses on educating lawmakers about mental illness and the need to improve and strengthen our mental health system. To make change. I am determined to fight for oversight, accountability, and evidence-based care in addressing all mental illnesses, not just eating disorders. I am desperate to make sure that there are no more Fantasy Islands.

I'm not sure I'm an activist yet, that I yearn for, but one goal in writing this book is to help me to achieve that end. I will always fight for reform and equity. Hell yeah!

My father and brother remain in a league of their own. They have always been there for me. No matter how hard as I pushed them away, their devotion was unwavering. Unconditional love was a mystery to me, always believing I was a disappointment, the ugly black sheep. My father and I didn't get along much while I was growing up, as my anorexia and depression were not understood by either of us. My eating disorder ruined so much. How could my father have possibly dealt with the erroneous accusations that he had abused me? He knew they weren't true, yet they almost destroyed my family. But my dad's love remained steadfast. He knew the truth.

My mom's love also remained steadfast, although I didn't always understand it. I raged at her for committing me to the psych ward at age 15, but I now realize that act saved my life.

Because of my illness, I lost my family's trust from my lies and reckless behavior. I stole a part of my brother's childhood as I was at war with myself and anyone who was in the way. A number of casualties left in my wake. It took a long time to regain their trust in me. Over time my father accepted my struggles and learned as much as he could about them. He still loves me, despite all we have been through. Devout in his religion and faith, attending church every morning. A man of integrity and character, courageous and kind. A man of his word, loyal and protective. I am very blessed.

My struggles have led me to develop my spiritual life. Believing in a higher power that I call God and using a conversational approach to prayer. Believing in faith, grace, and forgiveness, that we are all equal. Nurturing my spirit and soul through care for others. Believing in the purity of my actions, which are always a work in progress.

I have found much support from a book called *The Four Agreements* by Don Miguel Ruiz. The agreements he puts forth sounded sensible and powerful, but for a long time I didn't have enough clarity of thought to realize their power. Now I try to live by them every day. When practiced, they bring me to the present moment and closer to opening my heart.

BE IMPECCABLE WITH YOUR WORD

Speak with integrity. Say only what you mean. Avoid using the word to speak against yourself or to gossip about others. Use the power of your word in the direction of truth and love.

Words have tremendous power. They can trap me or set me free. Impeccable means in accordance with the highest standards; flawless. When I'm impeccable with my words, I'm accountable for my actions. It means I don't punish myself. Doing so will only keep me trapped in my fear and self-doubt.

I treat myself more kindly in my thoughts and I do not tell lies. I told too many in the past, trapped in my illness. My lies became a web that I couldn't escape. I thought little white lies were harmless, but of course that wasn't true. They were all too abundant when trying to hide my mental illness.

I use my words carefully. I have to be impeccable with them because my anorexia fills my head with constant self-criticism, doubt, and hatred. I have to be careful with my anger. I have to try to stop my constant berating of myself. My mom used to always tell me that if I didn't have anything good to say, to not say anything at all. And that includes how I speak to myself.

I have to be truthful even when it seems impossible. This is a challenge, because I can make excuses for my deficiencies. I can change how I deal with myself and how I deal with others.

The truth isn't always pretty. It may be subjective as well. I continue to learn my truth. Being impeccable with my word is the most powerful tool I have in continuing to grow and change.

DON'T TAKE ANYTHING PERSONALLY

Nothing others do is because of you. What others say and do is a projection of their own rules, their own dream. When you are immune to the opinions and actions of others, you won't be the victim of needless suffering.

I took everything personally. If someone looked at me the wrong way, I interpreted it as criticism. If someone complimented me, I was always skeptical. I always felt wronged, trying to be what I thought others expected of me. Letting them define me left me powerless and afraid, with a pain in my heart. I have to remind myself over and over again to never take anything personally.

Ruiz points out that doing so is the maximum expression of selfishness because we assume that everything is about "me." Wow, self-centered indeed. I had never looked at it that way. I was always paranoid that I'd done something wrong or that my shortcomings had caused the other person's reaction.

It's freeing to realize that what others do has nothing to do with me. It's about them. Even a direct insult doesn't define me. I will not accept another person's poison. Everyone has their own belief system that has nothing to do with me.

What a huge burden was taken off my shoulders when I learned not to take things personally. I only need to trust myself and follow my heart to make responsible choices.

DON'T MAKE ASSUMPTIONS

Find the courage to ask questions and to express what you really want. Communicate with others as clearly as you can to avoid misunderstandings, sadness, and drama. With just this one agreement, you can completely transform your life.

I made assumptions about almost everything and believed them to be true. For years I assumed if I lost more weight I would be happy. But now I'm learning to ask questions. Many questions. To not take anything at face value. It is so dangerous to make assumptions about ourselves. We create intense inner conflict from manufacturing false beliefs. Over time they became so difficult to unravel.

I'm learning to ask for what I want through good clear communication and by being in touch with my feelings.

Without making assumptions, we don't take things personally and our word becomes impeccable!

ALWAYS DO YOUR BEST

Your best is going to change from moment to moment; it will be different when you are healthy as opposed to sick. Under any circumstance, simply do your best, and you will avoid self-judgement, self-abuse, and regret.

My father always told me to simply do the best that I could. I never realized until recently the power in that advice. Perfection was always the goal. Anything less than perfection was a failure. Unattainable, as I learned after a lifetime of shame and self-hate from falling short. I now have a vision that embraces my imperfections. I'm learning from my mistakes. I'm managing my expectations. I'm not comparing my best to that of others. I'm doing the best to please myself and no one else.

My best can change from moment to moment. Sometimes it might simply be getting out of bed. Other times it's much more than that. Whether it's something small or something big, I try to avoid self judgement and self-hate. I do what I'm able to do. Period.

I spent too many years hiding from life and stuck in my head. Without taking action, I am not living. This is a very difficult challenge for me as hiding is my habit. I can only practice taking action and doing my best. I do mourn my many lost dreams because I was unable or unwilling to take action, whether it was because of fear or because of illness. I can forgive myself for hiding. I will not apologize for being sick. I did the best that I could. Period.

I may keep falling and falling, but I have to continue to try. It's so damn hard. So very difficult. I've lost many battles, but I feel I've won the war. I am taking it one day at a time. Just as I try to survive and heal—one day at a time. I want to live fully and finally be free to be me.

Epilogue

Forever in Blue Jeans

While I can see much better through the poisonous fog, it still looms quite thick. Thanks to amazing grace, I was able to see through that opening and tackle the fog that remains. I still have a ton of work to do to achieve the recovery I yearned for but never believed in. I now believe in it, without question or hesitation.

I remain afraid of grocery stores, restaurants and eating with people. I'm afraid of success and failure just the same. I fear uncertainty. My depression and anxiety are still there; as I continue my path to wellness, I will always have to learn to manage them. Coping skills I'm learning day after day.

I'm just learning, after decades of denial, that my emotions are authentic. They were suppressed for years by my eating disorder, not taken seriously by myself or by other people. Now I pay attention to them and investigate them and try to work with them, rather than running away from them. Experiencing them for what they are. They're not paranoia or delusions. I'm increasingly able to sit with them and not run away from them or distract myself from them, as hard as that might be. Feeling makes me vulnerable. Terrifying. But if I don't feel, I will never be free.

I have a disease. Several in fact. But I've learned that it wasn't my fault or a character flaw or an inherent weakness. Acceptance of my mental illness has come only in slow stages.

I can choose what I decide to focus on—the decades I lost to my eating disorder, or the comfort of the unconditional love from my family. I can mourn the loss of most of my life, or I can open my heart and accept the hope that others have for me. I can inspire critically needed change. But I can't do it alone. I need your help.

Thank the lord I have Hawkeye to remind me that he will not give up on me, that we are putting my puzzle pieces back together. Hawkeye reminds me over and over again of how far I've come. Showing me that I haven't wasted my life.

My successes may sound very simple. Learning how to feel. How to love and be loved. Getting out of bed in the morning. Getting out of the house. Advocating for better treatment options and education for people with EDs. Giving back. Writing this book. I have my purpose through small steps.

I often wonder who I could have become without my eating disorder. Without relentless depression and paralyzing anxiety. I had always wanted to make a difference with purpose.

Is it too late? Or is it better late than never? I have that opportunity now.

I'm blessed with friends who are there waiting for me to resurface whenever I disappear. Aware of the progress I have made and part of my support system. Invaluable. So forgiving and understanding, accepting me "as is" with humor and tears. These angels surround me and help me to survive. For better or for worse. In sickness and in health.

My mother's death has played an integral part in my recovery. She showed me that I had the strength to step up to the plate. If I could summon the strength to be with her at the end, I could summon that strength in other ways.

I wanted to be able to close this book with a celebration of personal transformation and full recovery. Closing my book with perfection, healed and happy.

But there will never be that perfect time. I will

always have mountains to climb. But what I can celebrate is my awareness, my acceptance of my journey, and my hard-won successes in my fight.

I have stopped apologizing for my illness, stopped apologizing for me. Taking it one step at a time. Not the number on the scale, not the car I drive, not the brand of my suit. Forever in blue jeans, I'm certain that's me.

No longer the performance driven by the expectations of others. To be free from the pressure that is no longer me. No more rubber chicken dinners. Not for yours truly. In my blue jeans forever—this is the life I want to lead.

I am reclaiming my power. My power of choice.

I can't change the past. I *can* change my attitude. I *can* change the present.

I can now see through a new lens. I can open my drapes. See the beauty of the trees in my back yard. Appreciate the power of the ocean. Not always hiding in darkness. Breathing fresh air. Enjoying a drive with no destination. Loving the wind blowing through my hair.

Acknowledgements

My Love.
My family and many cherished friends
(you know who you are).
You have stuck by me for better and for worse and
in sickness and in health. Hell yeah!
My current psychiatrist, for saving my life
and never giving up.
My editor, Al Desetta. Without his patience,
guidance, and expertise, I would have sunk.
And Neil Diamond, for being my Beethoven.

Sources

I have spent countless hours researching scholarly, medical, and psychiatric books, journals, articles, and organizations looking for answers. The list is far too extensive to cite in its entirety. Listed below are science-based resources to identify and disseminate clinically-sound policy, practices, and programs related to eating disorders. Statistical data mentioned in this book are derived from some of these sources.

Academy for Eating Disorders (AED)
    aedweb.org
American Journal of Psychiatry
    ajp.psychiatryonline.org
The Alliance for Eating Disorders Awareness
    allianceforeatingdisorders.com
American Medical Association (AMA)
    ama-assn.org
American Psychiatric Association (APA)
    psychiatry.org

American Psychological Association (APA)
   apa.org
Bazelon Center for Mental Health Law
   bazelon.org
Centers for Disease Control and Prevention (CDC)
   cdc.gov
Eating Disorders Coalition (EDC)
   eatingdisorderscoalition.org
Eating Disorder Hope
   eatingdisorderhope.com
Federal Bureau of Investigation (FBI).
   The FBI has conducted investigations into satanic cults.
   fbi.gov
Fast Facts on Eating Disorders
   aedweb.org
Frankfurter, David. *The Satanic Ritual Abuse Panic as Religious – Studies Data.* Law and Human Behavior, 2003.
The Kennedy Forum
   thekennedyforum.org
Mayo Clinic
   mayoclinic.org
Mental Health America
   mentalhealthamerica.net

Milliman

us.milliman.com

National Alliance on Mental Illness (NAMI)

nami.org

Nathan, D; Snedeker, M. *Satan's Silence: Ritual Abuse and the Making of a Modern American Witch Hunt.* Basic Books, 1995.

The National Association of Anorexia and Associated Disorders, Inc. (ANAD)

anad.org

National Association for Behavioral Healthcare: FKA as National Association of Psychiatric Health Systems

nabh.org

National Center for Biotechnology Information (NCBI)

ncbi.nim.nih.gov

National Center for Health Statistics (NCHS)

cdc.gov/nchs

National Eating Disorders Association (NEDA)

nationaleatingdisorders.org

National Institute of Health (NIH)

nih.gov

National Institute of Mental Health (NIMH)

nimh.gov

National Vital Statistics System (NVSS)

cdc.gov/nchs/nvss

Ofshe, Richard; Watters, Ethan. *Making Monsters: False Memories, Psychotherapy, and Sexual Hysteria.* New York, London, Toronto, Sydney, Tokyo, Singapore: Charles Scribner's Sons, 1994.

Office of the Attorney General
justice.gov/ag

Office of the Surgeon General (OSG)
hhs.gov

Pendergrast, Mark. *The Repressed Memory Epidemic: How It Happened and What We Need to Learn from It.* Switzerland: Springer International Publishing AG, 2017.

Prasad, K. *Fundamentals of Evidence–Based Medicine.* New Delhi, Pa.: Meeta Publishers, 2005.

Ruiz, Don Miguel. *The Four Agreements.* San Rafael, Ca.: Amber – Allen Publishing, 1997.

Social Security Administration (SSA)
ssa.gov

Substance Abuse Mental Health Services Administration (SAMHSA) samhsa.gov

U.S. Department of Commerce
commerce.gov

U.S. Department of Health and Human Services (HHS)
hhs.gov

U.S. Department of Justice (DOJ)
justice.gov

U.S. Food and Drug Administration (FDA)
fda.gov

U.S. National Library of Medicine (NLM)
nim.nih.gov

Victor, J.S. *Satanic Panic: The Creation of a Contemporary Legend.* Open Court Publishing Company, 1993.

World Health Organization (WHO)
who.int

Made in United States
North Haven, CT
13 August 2023

40269493R20121